LIPAN WARRIOR

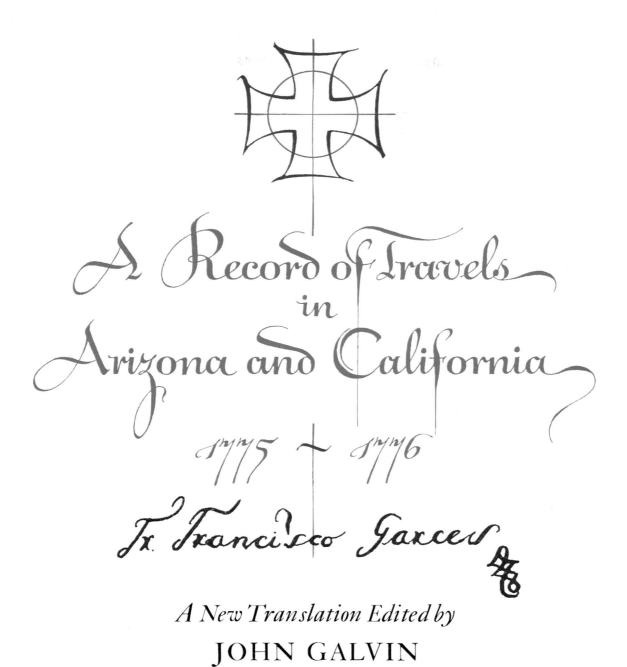

A Record of Travels in Arizona and California

1775 ~ 1776

Fr. Francisco Garcés

A New Translation Edited by

JOHN GALVIN

PUBLISHED BY JOHN HOWELL—BOOKS
MCMLXV

This book may be used in whole or in part by anyone who wishes to do so, with the Editor's compliments, for no copyright exists on this work.

PUBLISHED BY JOHN HOWELL—BOOKS
434 POST STREET · SAN FRANCISCO

Library of Congress Catalogue Card No. 65-23988
Printed in the United States of America

1250 COPIES
DESIGNED AND PRINTED BY LAWTON AND ALFRED KENNEDY
SAN FRANCISCO

For Mother

PREFATORY NOTE

THE TRANSLATION presented in this volume is Father Garcés' record of his long-est and most important journey in the American Southwest, a journey that occupied eleven months in 1775-1776. I have used a contemporary manuscript copy in my library. The manuscript is of thirty-two numbered leaves, 8½ by 12 inches in size, all closely written on both sides except the last, which has only four lines written at the top of the recto side. In the last line it has as colophon: "Tubutama y Enero 3 de 1777. Fr. Franco Garces," the author's name being copied, not a signature. The handwriting of the copyist through-out is clear and even, and the work has few scribal errors.

Several other contemporary manuscript copies are known. There are at least three in the National Archives of Mexico. A copy from Mexico is in the Archive of the Indies, in Spain, and another is in the central Franciscan archive in Rome. The copy from which Elliott Coues made his translation into English, published in 1900, was in the Library of the Bureau of American Ethnology at Washington, D. C., which received it from a Mexican scholar, Dr. Nicolás León. Coues also had under his hand another manuscript then (1897) belong-ing to Dr. León, of which the latter wrote: "Appears to have been made in or for the archives of the Convento de la Cruz de Querétaro by Padre Fray de la Purísima Concepción Beaumont, who died in 1779." This last-mentioned manuscript has as colophon, according to Coues, "En Tubutama. I. de enero de 1777. Fr. Franco Garces." Other copies, so far as I am aware, name the same place and author but give the date as the 3rd, not the 1st, of January, except that one gives the 30th.

There is also a printed version in Spanish: "Diario y derecho que siguió el M. R. P. Fr. Francisco Garcés en su viage hecho desde Octubre de 1775 hasta 17 de Setiembre de 1776, al Río Colorado para reconocer las naciones que habitan sus márgenes, y á los pueblos del Moqui del Nuevo-México," occupy-ing pages 225-374 in *Documentos para la historia de México*, second series, Volume I (Mexico City, 1854).

The history and fate of the original holograph, if Father Garcés wrote with his own hand and did not dictate his Diario, seem not to have been reported. The various copies of the manuscript show some variations. The printed ver-sion has the most, whether because it was changed by its publishers or tran-scribes a manuscript now lost. The copy in my library seems to be one of the final group of fair copies prepared, probably with revision by Father Garcés, for submission to the Spanish Crown.

The present translation was first undertaken by the late Miss Adelaide Smithers. To all others who have helped me I give grateful acknowledgement, and particular thanks to Dr. Woodrow Borah, Professor Roger McHugh, and Mr. Harold A. Small for their interest and kindness, and to Dr. A. R. Orme and Mrs. Adrienne E. Morgan for their aid with my maps. For many courtesies I am indebted to the Bancroft Library and its director, Dr. George P. Hammond.

J.G.

TABLE OF CONTENTS

LIST OF ILLUSTRATIONS

The portrayal of the Virgin of Guadalupe is from a sermon printed in Mexico City in 1751; color devised by Paul Q. Forster. The drawing of the old garrison chapel at Tubac and the vignettes used at the head of sections of Father Garcés' account are the work of Adrienne Morgan, and the calligraphy is by Albert Meakin.

INTRODUCTION

FATHER GARCÉS, who received at baptism the names of three saints, Francisco, Tomás, and Hermenegildo, was born on April 12, 1738, in the town of Morata del Conde, in Aragón. He was beaten to death on July 19, 1781, when hostile Indians fell upon two small mission-posts on the lower Colorado River and killed all four of the missionary priests there.

He was a Franciscan. Ordained a priest at the age of twenty-five, he entered at twenty-eight a seminary for missionaries, the Colegio de la Santa Cruz, at Querétaro, Mexico, and at thirty he was sent to the frontier mission of San Xavier del Bac in what is now southern Arizona. Tucson, the nearest present-day place of importance, was then a deserted Indian ranchería, and the mission building at Bac—as San Xavier del Bac was often called—was a modest adobe structure not at all comparable with the splendid edifice, built a generation later, that still startles the gaze of the traveller. Beyond Bac there were as yet no white men; it would be several years before Garcés could mention Tucson as "the last Christian settlement" on the northern frontier. Bac was on the very edge of hostile Indian country.

From Bac, Garcés made a number of journeys into the lands of the Indians to the west and north: in 1768 he visited the Pápagos, nearest west, and went up to the Gila River, and while he was away and stricken with a sudden illness the Apaches plundered his mission; in 1770 he went again to the Gila River and to the Opas; in 1771 he went further west and reached the Colorado, which he followed to its mouth on the Gulf of California; early in 1774 he accompanied a small expedition under Captain Juan Bautista de Anza to San Gabriel Mission in southern California; the next year, starting with the second and much larger expedition led by Anza, who was now promoted lieutenant-colonel, he branched off by himself and made the extensive travels described in the present day-to-day Record; and in 1779 he visited his old friends the Yumas, who lived at the confluence of the Gila and Colorado rivers. He was a memorable traveller in the interest of both church and state.

Father Garcés began his longest and most noteworthy journey on October 21, 1775, and ended it on September 17, 1776, having made his way over more than two thousand miles of desert, mountain, and riverland terrain. His first duties, as a missionary, were to learn which of the Indian tribes were ready to receive religious instruction, and to teach them the rudiments of the Faith. He had also to report which of the tribes—presumably the same ones—were ready to become subjects of the King of Spain. And in accordance with instructions from the Viceroy of New Spain he had an eye open all the way for an overland route that would link the Province of Sonora and the Colorado River country with Monterey and San Francisco, respectively the most important and the most recent Spanish establishments on the Pacific coast in Upper California. He reported his findings in detail. The Viceroy was pleased, and told him the King was pleased. And we are all in his debt, for his account is a landmark in the history of that wide region.

The start was easy. Riding south from his mission to the garrison-post of Tubac, some thirty-five miles distant, he joined the expedition and found it well supplied and with an ample guard of soldiers. The way north and northwest to the Gila River was familiar. After nine days of travel the expedition halted to rest, and Father Garcés and others made a side excursion to see the ruin of the Casa Grande, which even then was mistakenly called "the Great House of Moctezuma." Later, on his return journey, Garcés visited the Hopi Indian country, remembered the designs on the potsherds at the great ruin, and correctly saw a relationship between them and the pottery of the Hopis. Thus he was something of an archaeologist, perhaps a better one than those who spoke of "Aztec ruins."

At the beginning of December the expedition, travelling west, reached the Colorado River and thence departed for California, handing over to Garcés and his colleague Father Tomás Eixarch a not over-large store of supplies, and, for company, "a little boy, two Spaniards [of whom he says no more], three interpreters, and another Indian." Leaving Eixarch to prepare the Yumas for mission life, Garcés at once set off independently. On his travels he generally had for company a few friendly Indians, but always different ones because tomorrow's Indians might not be friendly with today's. The scheme of interpretation also was progressive, the Indians of one place knowing something of the language of their neighbours but not necessarily of any language spoken further away. In very few places could Garcés himself speak the local tongue. For giving the heathen some notion of Christian doctrine he had to rely partly on signs and partly on the dramatic use of appeals to the eye. He used the Christ on his crucifix, pictures in his breviary, and a canvas painted on both sides, one side showing the Virgin Mary and the other a damned man (presumably in the torments of hellfire). He also chanted a hymn or prayer from his service book; the Indians, he says, like to "see him pray and sing."

Then there was the daily problem of subsistence; travel meant going from one watering-place to another and eating whatever the Indians or nature might offer. Father Garcés tells over and over again of "giving presents" to the Indians and of their "regaling" him, which means that in exchange for a little tobacco or a few beads they would give him a part of such food as they had. When he ran out of gifts he was embarrassed to accept hospitality, no matter how scant. At times his fare was thin indeed. The preacher of a sermon honouring the memory of Garcés, among others, tells us, as the traveller himself does not, that "mice and small lizards" were on the menu; this may have been an orator's flourish, but then again it may not. Once, in the extremity of hunger, Garcés and his Indian companions fed on the flesh and blood of a slaughtered horse, and he adds that rationing was necessary if they were to reach the next inhabited place. Delicacies were rare; to him, a few ripe melons were nectar and ambrosia.

When he set out he had a quadrant and a compass. In one of the manuscript copies of his Record (not the one used here) he says that he made his last observation of latitude when, having crossed the Tehachapi Mountains, he was heading north in the great valley of California; but what became of the quadrant he does not tell. He lost the compass needle in ground riddled by kangaroo rats, on his way south again. He always specified in what direction he travelled, and set down how many leagues he went. The distances he gives are sometimes in fair accord with modern land measurements, sometimes not. His estimates were often dependent upon the footing and rate of advance made by his mount; an hour's plodding was a league.

He always took note of landmarks—mountains, rivers, lesser watercourses wet or dry, marshes, sand dunes—that are helps to the recording or retracing of a path once taken. When he gave names to such things, or to Indians' dwelling-places, like other Spanish missionary-explorers he commonly honoured the saint whose day it happened to be, as, on April 25, naming a mountain range (the Tehachapi) for St. Mark; or he would use a familiar reference, as for example the Nativity, or the Wounds *(Las Llagas)* which were repeated in the stigmata of St. Francis.

He mentioned, by their commonest collective names, the presence of trees. But he says nothing of reptiles and little of other living creatures: of birds, that he once saw cranes and crows; of insects, once, wasps; of fishes, only to name the one kind taken in the Gila River that is worth eating, if the eater can escape its many bones; or of wild animals, except to remark that some of the mountain

Indians fear the bears, and to reflect that what some Indians had offered him as a chunk of meat, possibly the head of one of his own mules which had been left behind, must after all have been the head of a buffalo. Buffalo? He uses the common name for the animal, though in the feminine form, *cíbola;* but were there any buffaloes where he went, or did he mean the female of some other species? Rabbits, hares, and squirrels he mentions only as eatables; otters, for their fur; kangaroo rats, as a nuisance. He was no naturalist.

On his return journey he saw the Grand Canyon of the Colorado. He did not attempt to describe its wonders. In need of water and food, he made his way to a community of friendly Indians at the very bottom of a deep side-canyon by taking the same route which, two generations later, Lieutenant Joseph C. Ives of the U. S. Army described (and his is a hair-raising description still). For once, Garcés was jarred out of his usual plodding style and common vocabulary. To find a name for the place where the trail led along a "narrow way some three handbreadths wide, with a very high cliff on one side and on the other a hideous abyss," he resorted in memory to Spain and called it "the new Canfran," after a pass in the high Pyrenees between his native Aragón and Béarn; and the way up again out of the depths, notwithstanding that he had benefitted from food and rest as the Indians had kept him for several days, he called a "most painful ascent," its precipices "horrifying."

Aside from remarking that, at certain places, the earth is red, or the water red or yellow, or, once only, that the bands of rock exposed in a pass are varicoloured, he said nothing of the brilliantly painted landscapes through which he passed. One hesitates to judge that he was insensitive to them; perhaps he was surfeited with the strong colours of the Southwest.

After the Grand Canyon, he went into the land of the Hopi Indians, who would have nothing to do with him. From there he went home to his mission of San Xavier del Bac.

As an observer of Indians he had a sharp and knowing eye. He recorded a large number of details, enlarging the Spaniards' knowledge of Indian life; and the modern ethnologist, too, has learned from him.

It is from his own recital of his relations with the Indians that one best sees Garcés himself, a hardy, generous, essentially warmhearted man. His approach to the heathen was direct and friendly. He was on the best of terms with his fellow priests, and he seems to have got along well enough with the Spanish military—at least, he speaks well of Anza, as Father Font does not. He quarrelled with no one; or if he did, he kept it out of his account. He came near an altercation with the military commander in California, Rivera, at San Gabriel; but then, differences between Spanish officers and missionary priests were not rare.

Father Garcés was a devoted priest; at the end of his life, a martyr. He was a pathfinder worthy of remembrance, an indefatigable traveller, uncomplaining under stress of hardship, bold under challenge. In sum, he is one of the most attractive and respectable figures in all the early history of the Southwest.

THE RECORD OF TRAVELS

GARRISON CHAPEL, TUBAC PRESIDIO

Diario que hà formado el Padre

Fr. Francisco Garcés

A Daily Record prepared by Father Francisco Garcés, a son of the Colegio de la Santa Cruz, Querétaro, of the journey made in this year 1775 by order of His Excellency Antonio María Bucareli y Ursua, Lieutenant-General, Viceroy, Governor, and Captain-General of this New Spain, as made known in his letter of January 2 of the said year and decided upon by the Council of War held in Mexico City on November 28 of the year preceding; and by order likewise of the Rev. Father Romualdo Cartagena, Guardián of the said Colegio, in his letter of January 20, 1775; and in another letter by his successor the Rev. Father Diego Ximénez, of February 17 of the same year, in which I was directed, together with another religious, to join Lieutenant-Colonel Juan Bautista de Anza and the Rev. Father Pedro Font, who were to go to the harbour of San Francisco, accompanying them as far as the Colorado River, where with my companion I was to await their return and in the meantime to look over the country and treat with the near-by Indian nations, determining if they were disposed and ready for religious instruction and for becoming subjects of our Sovereign.

PRELIMINARY REMARKS

THERE ACCOMPANIES this Record a map made by Father Font with the greatest care and while I was at his side so that I might give him, in addition to the data herein, other information that should help to ensure its accuracy. The latitudes observed, compass directions, and leagues travelled which I have set down as far as the Laguna de Santa Eulalia agree with those of Father Font's diary and map; I was in his company as far as the Colorado River and afterward saw him again at the Laguna. The rest I made with a quadrant he lent me. Owing to my lack of practice probably not all of them are exact. On the map the entire route is shown by dots, and [in the Record] the length of each day's journey is given in numbers for greater clarity. Also the [areas with] names of the Indian nations are set off with little marks for better understanding of the direction in which each one lies from another and how far they extend. However, some of these areal limits are based only on the best judgement that could be made.

After seeing such a variety of nations and learning about their friendships, wars, and trade (not in one place alone: one item of information would be gathered from one nation, another from another, and from what some Indians would tell me and what I myself might see in one nation I would understand what in another had not been told me), it seemed best to me, once the Record was completed, to give separate information about each of these nations, and, joining together all the data that I have acquired, to show the connection that some nations have with others; which are the dominant ones; which are friends and which are enemies; what their trade is; what their territorial extent; and finally, as a consequence of everything, to propose the means, inferrible from all that I have seen, that may be most useful toward the desired end, which is the total submission of the Apache nation and communication between Monterey, New Mexico, and these provinces.

In compliance with orders, Father Tomás Eixarch was appointed to be my companion.

Since I saw that in no way could I explain things better to the Indians than with pictures of such sort that they would understand them at sight, I decided to take with me a canvas on one side of which was a painting of Mary Most Holy with the Divine Child in her arms, and on the other a painting of a damned man. I had noticed that on every occasion of my going into heathen territory the Holy Crucifix that hung at my breast excited devotion in the Indians and that they always adored it, acknowledging to me that it was a good thing—as will be seen from what I am going to relate.

Non fecit taliter omni nation

Troncoso.exc.

Oct. 21   *1st day of journey*

1775   I went to the Presidio of Tubac with my companion Father Tomás Eixarch, and with Father Pedro Font, to join the commander of the expedition, Lieutenant-Colonel Juan Bautista de Anza.

Oct. 22   A Mass was sung beseeching the favour of Mary Most Holy, under her title as Virgin of Guadalupe, who had been chosen patroness of the expedition. I celebrated Mass in honour of St. Peter the Apostle, who is my special patron in this and all my other goings into heathen territory.

    The Rev. Father Pedro [Font] took an observation at this presidio and found the latitude to be 31° 43′.

Oct. 23   *2nd day*   *Leagues travelled 5*
We left the Presidio of Tubac and halted at a place called Canoa; to reach it we travelled five leagues in a northeast direction.

Oct. 24   *3rd day*   *6*
We left Canoa and stopped at the edge of Los Llanos [the Flats], having gone six leagues northeast by north.

Oct. 25   *4th day*   *6*
We arrived at my Mission of San Xavier del Bac, having travelled six leagues in the same direction.

Oct. 26   *5th day*   *4*
We arrived at a watering-place outside of Tucson, which is the last Christian settlement in this direction and is included in my pastorate. The distance travelled was four leagues almost due north.

Oct. 27   *6th day*   *5*
Father Font took an observation at this place and found it to be at 32° 22′. We left it in the afternoon and halted at a flat within sight of the mountain range called La Frente Negra ['The Dark Face'; the Tucson Mountains]. We had travelled five leagues, two northnorthwest and three northwest.

Oct. 28   *7th day*   *6*
We halted at some rain pools called by the Indians Oitapars near which there was once a village of the Pápago Indians, who left it a

few years ago because of raids by the Apaches. We had travelled six long leagues west-northwest with occasional deviations to the west.

Oct. 29   *8th day*   *5*

We arrived near the ranchería of Quitoac, where at times some Pápagos live, and halted a little beyond a butte which the Indians call Tacca. We had travelled two leagues northwest and three north-northwest. This same day a messenger was sent to notify the Gileño Pimas of our coming. The Commander, with his sure sense of what was fitting,[1] directed the proclaiming of an order by which all members of the expedition were admonished that in no way were they to set a bad example to the heathen, much less offend them in the slightest by deed or word, on pain of severe punishment to offenders.

Oct. 30   *9th day*   *12*

We neared the Gila River and halted at a watering-place after travelling twelve leagues, six northwest, three north-northwest, and three north. On the way we saw no pasturage, but to one or the other side off our road there is enough. The Gileño Pimas came out to meet us as a result of yesterday's message; that is, the governors of the two rancherías called Aquituni and Quitoa, the governor of Utidituc, with its alcalde, accompanied also by the governor of Sutaquisón, and many other Indians on horseback, who dismounted to greet us. They gave the soldiers the scalps of two Apaches they had killed a few days before; with those Indians they carry on much warfare. They remounted and escorted us to where they live. They kept asking us repeatedly if we were finally coming to live with them and to baptize them, which seemed to me a sign that these Indians are very well disposed toward Christian teaching. They all showed great joy over our coming.

Oct. 31   The Commander decided that the expedition should rest. Therefore we went to see the large structure that is called the House of Mocte-

---

1. On the two occasions when he says anything specific about Anza, Garcés speaks well of him. This professional soldier, whose father before him had been an army officer in Sonora province, led two expeditions from Tubac to San Gabriel with conspicuous success. Afterward, he was for ten years both civil and military governor of New Mexico. He is remembered in California by the Anza Desert State Park, in an area through which he passed; by Lake Anza, in a part of the State he never saw; and by a post office.

zuma, travelling for that purpose three leagues west-southwest. The site is at 33° 3 ½'. As to the position and arrangement of this structure, I refer to the description given by Father Font.[2] At the end of the present Record I shall set down my own conjectures as a consequence of what I have seen and heard in Moqui.

Nov. 1   *10th day*   *4*

We left the watering-place and after travelling four leagues west-northwest we came to the ranchería of San Juan Capistrano, where we were received by about a thousand Indians drawn up in two lines. For our reception they had contrived a large arbour and had set up in front of it a cross. As soon as we dismounted they came over to greet us, kissing our hands and uttering the name of God, as those other Pimas do who are Christians.

Whenever we have been with these poor heathen they have received me always with the same affection, and I have regretted not being able to fulfil the great desire they show to be Christians; but on this occasion I was the more distressed at seeing so many gathered together who wanted us to stay there to baptize them. In gentleness, pleasantness of manner, and aptitude for living together in their villages they surpass all others of their nation. Yet, even so, the time does not seem to have come for bringing these souls within the fold of the Church. May God so dispose as and when it may please Him most.

They took care of our wants and feasted us extravagantly, for they have sheep very like those of the Hopi Indians or perhaps the same; I shall speak of them at the end of this Record. They have chickens; horses, also, some of which they bartered with the soldiers for baize. They brought us the drinking-water needed for all of us and they served us in everything just as might be expected from old Christians and very faithful subjects of the King. Tobacco and beads were distributed to them.

---

2. Father Font, after returning from this expedition, greatly expanded his travel notes, and in the expanded account he included in his entry for October 31, 1775, a detailed description of the Casa Grande ruin. He gave the direction from camp as east-southeast, which seems preferable to Garcés' "west-southwest."

[7]

After we three priests had celebrated on this Day of the Dead the nine Masses, which were heard by some of the Indians, we went four leagues west by north and halted on the banks of the Gila River near the village called La Encarnación del Sutaquisón. The Indians of this village, numbering perhaps five hundred at the most, came out to meet us with signs of pleasure.

In the region of these four leagues one comes upon the villages[3] of Atisón, Tubus Cabors, and San Serafín de Napcub, which is on the other bank of the river. At this village of La Encarnación de Sutaquisón ends the Pima nation of the Gila River, which in the region of four leagues has five villages: San Juan Capistrano de Uturituc, San Andrés de Tubus Cabors, Atisón, San Serafín de Napcub, and La Encarnación de Sutaquisón, which have altogether, I judge, about two thousand five hundred souls. All these villages have large sowings of wheat, and some of maize, cotton, squash, and other seed crops. For irrigation they have dug good channels. The fields are surrounded by a common fence, and those of the separate owners are set off each by its own fence. These Indians go clothed in blankets that they themselves make from cotton or from the wool of their sheep or wool brought from Moqui. This part of the day's journey hasn't much forage, but in the village called Sutaquisón there is enough to keep a presidio supplied, as Captain Bernardo de Urrea reported after he made a personal inspection of the most appropriate sites for founding missions.

In the same village of Sutaquisón, and in that of San Juan Capistrano, I showed the Indians the picture of Mary Most Holy and that of the Damned Man. I preached to them in their language, which is the same as that of my village.

My companion Father Tomás and I went over from this place to Sutaquisón to distribute tobacco and beads. After returning to the camping-place, and having gone two leagues northwest, we came to pools of bad water that had caused some sickness and so were called

---

3. In the manuscript the information is given twice, perhaps by a copyist's error; nevertheless it seems best to keep the repetition in the translation.

the Lagunas del Hospital. To the west of these pools is the Sierra de San José de Comars [the Sierra Estrella], which ends at the Gila River near the place where the Asunción [the Salt River] joins it. This latter river is much larger than the Gila; it rises a great deal in the summer as the snow-masses melt in the mountains in which it rises and through which it flows. I shall say more about it at the end of this Record. I found this place to be at 33° 14½'. We stayed here the 4th, 5th, and 6th.

Nov. 7   *13th day*   *6*
We left the Lagunas del Hospital and, having travelled six leagues, one southeast, two west-southwest, and three west, we stopped at a waterless arroyo. In all these six leagues there is plenty of pasturage but no water.

Nov. 8   *14th day*   *9*
We travelled nine leagues, two west-southwest, one west to go through a pass in the mountains, and the rest west-southwest with some inclination to the west. We came to the village of the Holy Apostles Sts. Simon and Jude [near Gila Bend], which is of the Opa or Cocomaricopa nation (it is all one). They received us with much pleasure. About a thousand gathered in this village to see us and we distributed tobacco and beads among them. Here the Indians have all kinds of seed and as a rule gather two harvests, depending on rainfall; but, as we saw, they can also run an irrigation channel from the river, which because it is joined further up by the Asunción has plenty of water at all times.

Most of these Indians are clothed like the Gileño Pimas, whose very good friends and companions they are in the campaigns they both carry on against the Tejua Yavipais, of whom I shall speak later. Having shown them the Virgin and the Damned Man, I preached to them through an interpreter because their language is not Pima but Yuma. I asked them if they wished with all their hearts to be Christians and to admit the missionary priests to their lands and they answered, with great pleasure, yes. We stayed here on the 9th and 10th.

[9]

Nov. 11 *15th day*   *2*

We went about two leagues west and came to a ranchería of Opa Indians which was near the river.

Nov. 12 *16th day*   *5*

After five leagues we reached, near the river, a group of rancherías of the same nation, which we called San Diego. Our direction was west by north.

Nov. 13 *17th day*   *4*

Going four leagues west by south, we arrived at a place called Aritoac, having crossed the river a little way before coming to it.

Nov. 14 *18th day*   *4*

Having travelled four leagues to the west-southwest,[4] we reached Agua Caliente. Near this place are the rancherías called after San Bernardino, and the people are of the same [Opa] nation. About two hundred came to visit us. I showed them the paintings and preached to them, putting to them the question: Did they wish to be baptized and to have missionary priests live in their lands? They answered yes. I urged the old men to gather the people together so that the Commander might select from among them, in the King's name, a governor and an alcalde. An old man answered me, very seriously, with these words: "Look here, a magistrate's duty is to punish evil, and as we are not bad why the magistrate? You Spaniards have already seen that we are not thievish, not quarrelsome, and even if we are near a woman we do nothing wrong." My faith in their goodness does not extend so far, although this Opa nation is quite as worthy as the Pima. When I asked them what knowledge they had of their ancestors, they answered more or less like the Gileños with respect to the Flood and Creation, as the Commander and Father Font tell in their account, and added that their origin was near the sea, where an old woman created their progenitors; that this old woman is still somewhere (nobody knows where); that

---

4. The manuscript gives, as the direction, *oest sudeste*, 'west-southeast', which is contrary to sense; and similar oddities occur in the opening lines of the entries for April 13 *(est norueste,* 'east-northwest'), May 30 and July 1 *(est sudoeste,* 'east-southwest'), and July 5 *(est norueste,* 'east-northwest' again). In the translation each of these has been silently brought into accord with the dictates of the passage in which it occurs.

it is she who sends the corals from the same sea; that when they die their hearts go to live by the sea, toward the west; that some, after they die, live as owls; and finally they said that they did not know these things well, that those who did know them well are the ones living in the mountain range beyond the Colorado River. The Commander named a governor and an alcalde, and they were very proud, saying that now their names would reach the King. Perhaps it was this that inclined them to show off in the presence of Captain Palma.[5]

The Opa or Cocomaricopa nation—it is all one—ends here, though some of these Indians are nevertheless found further downstream. It seems to me that they number about three thousand. We were sensible that the peace with the Yuma nation which we had brought about on our former expedition was continuing. To ensure it further, some of the Opas went downriver with us to that nation, where, with great rejoicing on both sides, and to our comfort, the peace was confirmed. Among its other good results is an end to the very many deaths that both sides used to suffer. From this place word of our arrival was sent to the Jalchedun nation so that without misgivings those Indians could come down to celebrate peace with the Yumas.

This place was found to be at 33° 2½'. We stayed here on the 15th.

Nov. 16   *19th day*   *9*
Nine leagues west-southwest and we came near the Colorado River [*sic;* the Gila River is meant]. Its bed is very wide here.

Nov. 17   *20th day*   *2*
Two leagues in the same direction and we reached the [Gila] river.

Nov. 18   *21st day*   *4*
Travelling four leagues southwest, we stopped on the bank of the river at the foot of the Cerro de San Pasqual. This place is at 32°48'. Here we stayed on the 19th, 20th, and 21st.

Nov. 22   *22nd day*   *6*
Continuing six leagues southwest, we came to the hill called by the

5. Captain Palma was a Yuma chieftain, friendly to the Spaniards and favoured by them.

Indians the Cerro del Metate and named by us after St. Cecilia.[6]
Here we stopped on the 23rd and 24th.

Nov. 25   *23rd day*   *5*
Going five leagues west by north, we halted beside a brackish pool.
A Yuma Indian sent by Captain Palma came to assure us that all
the people were eagerly awaiting our arrival. From here the Cocomaricopa magistrates who were with us went off to the Yumas.

Nov. 26   *24th day*   *4*
After travelling four leagues northwest we stopped at the bank of
the river.

Nov. 27   *25th day*   *2*
Going two leagues west-northwest, we halted in a pass through
which the river flows in a very narrow channel. A brother of
Captain Palma came here to meet us, and later Palma and his brother
Pablo arrived, showing great joy, especially the former, who went
around embracing all our people.

Nov. 28   *26th day*   [*5*]
Having forded the Gila River and travelled five leagues west by
south, we stopped at a shelter of branches that Captain Palma had
ordered made. Many Indians, both men and women, came in a
happy manner and, in the presence of all, peace was confirmed
between the two nations, Cocomaricopa and Yuma. About a league
below this region, which in my earlier accounts I call San Pedro de
los Yumas, the Gila River joins the Colorado. The Gila, so far as
I have been able to learn on my journeys, rises in the Sierra de
Mogollón and runs, in the main, east to west, although at Uparsoitac
it changes direction to the west-southwest. In its course there are
added to it the San Juan Nepomuceno, the San Pedro, the San Carlos
(undoubtedly that which in older writings is called the San Francisco), and the Asunción, which is composed of the Verde and the
Salado. The Gila receives the larger part of its waters from the
Asunción, which rises greatly with the melting of the snows of the
mountain ranges through which it passes. On the banks of the Gila

---

6. A *metate* is a stone for grinding cornmeal by hand. Presumably the hill was seen
to resemble such a stone. November 22 is St. Cecilia's day.

are cottonwoods, willows, and mesquites. Along this river there is little pasturage, but in the ranchería of San Andrés, now abandoned, and in the vicinity of Sutaquisón there is some fodder, and everywhere there is an abundance of bushes and common reed-grass. No other fish is found in this river than the one they call *matalote* ['scrawny old nag'], which though tasty is vexing because it is so full of bones.

By this river is found the house that is said to be Moctezuma's, and numerous ruins of other buildings; also very many fragments of earthenware, some with coloured designs and others not, and because of what I later saw of Moqui I have since formed an opinion very different from the one I then had about these products.

Nov. 29   This day was spent in seeking a path and opening a way through the dense thickets of the Colorado River and then finding a ford where the expedition could cross.

Nov. 30   *27th day*   *1*

The Cocomaricopa magistrates took leave of us and went back to their land. The entire expedition crossed the Colorado without any mishap, and, having gone on perhaps a league to the northwest, stopped on the shore of the same river. We had crossed at a place where it is divided in three branches; I estimated the width as about four hundred varas,[7] for it was now very low. When it rises, it extends for leagues.

Dec. 1   The Commander, Father Tomás, and I myself went with some muleteers to Captain Palma's dwelling-place, about a league to the west of our camp, to build a hut that was to serve us [i.e., the two priests] as a lodging until the return of the expedition. This night Captain Palma wore the suit of clothes given him by the Viceroy as a present in thanks to him for the good service he has rendered the Spaniards. On this same night three or four Jalchedun women came with one man to say, on behalf of their people, that they were determined to make peace with the Yumas because of the message we had sent them. Moreover, we also heard this night, in the man's talk, an odd story. After we had asked him many questions about his coun-

---

7.   A *vara* (Spanish yard) equals about 33 inches; hence, about 360 yards.

[13]

try, he told us among other things that there was a man there who had come from the new missions in California; he had been killed and reduced to ashes by the nations through which he had passed: but that he had the power to turn himself into a whirlwind; that he carried with him a viper, and was a great wizard; that he could make the Jalcheduns do what he wanted and therefore they were much in awe of him. Our Commander showed some vexation, even in spite of the very great patience he has with the Indians—a trait worthy of being imitated by all who are sent on such enterprises. I asked him for some beads, which I gave to these Indians.

Dec. 2   I continued building the hut with the Lieutenant [Moraga]. The Indians helped a little, and beads were given to those who worked. On this day tobacco was distributed to all the Yuma men, and beads to all the women, who came there.

Dec. 3   The hut was completed and the expedition reached this place. The Commander delivered to Father Tomás and me the supplies he was leaving for our subsistence.[8]

Dec. 4   The expedition set out for its destination, leaving as our company six persons: a little boy, two Spaniards, and three interpreters on the expedition's rolls. These with another Indian lent us by Captain Bernardo Urrea made a total of seven.

---

8. Father Garcés does not say how much of these provisions he took with him as he set out on his independent travels; it can hardly have been more than a pack load or so. The articles left for him and Father Eixarch, as other accounts tell, were tobacco and glass beads (to give to Indians), chocolate, sugar, flour, lard, hardbread, dried beef, (dried) chickpeas, hams, cheeses, soap, candles, a frying pan, a flat earthenware pan (for cooking tortillas), an axe or hatchet, five beeves on the hoof, and a jug of bad wine.

[Yuma Crossing to Mouth of the Colorado]

Dec. 5 *28th day of journey* *Leagues travelled 5*

Seeing that the weather was very favourable for visiting the nations of the Colorado River as far as its mouth and inquiring into their disposition toward religious instruction, which is what the Viceroy ordered me to do, I decided to set out for this purpose. I put aside what I was to give them, and taking with me the Indian Sebastián Taraval and the other two interpreters I left after saying good-bye to my well-beloved companion. Having travelled five leagues west-southwest, I stopped at the first of the San Pablo rancherías. I spoke to the people and showed them the painting of Mary Most Holy and that of the Damned Man; and they said to me that that Lady was good and the damned soul very bad; that they were not so foolish as not to know that the good people are up in Heaven, and down inside the earth are the bad people, dogs, and horrible wild beasts. They knew all this because the Pimas had told them of it. I offered to their consideration: Did they wish the priests and Spaniards to come to live in their country? They answered yes, they would be very glad of that since they would have meat and a means of covering their nakedness. I distributed tobacco and beads and left them well content.

Dec. 6 *29th day* *10*

I travelled ten leagues southwest, now and then turning aside to visit some rancherías to the west or south. Arriving at the Laguna de Santa Eulalia, I met the Commander with Father Font and all the expedition. At this place were many of the mountain Indians whom the Yumas call Quemeyás. They wear sandals of maguey fibre as a protection against stones, and come down to this region to eat squash and other products of the bottomlands. They live in the mountains among the Indians of San Jacomé, San Sebastián, and even as far as San Diego. The Yuma nation ends in these rancherías.

Dec. 7 I stopped at the Laguna de Santa Eulalia, as did the Commander, Father Font, and the rest of the expedition. This place is at 32° 33′. Here begins the territory of the Cajuenches, many of whom were gathered together, but not all, and therefore I cannot say how many they are. I distributed tobacco and beads. Showing them the portrayals of Mary Most Holy and the Damned Man, I gave them to hear of the things of God, at which they showed great rejoicing, crying to the Divine Lady that all was very good; but the Damned Man so filled them with horror that they shouted their unwillingness to look at it, and they would make me turn the painting round. They added that they very much wanted the Fathers and the Spaniards to come to their lands.

At this watering-place and in the surrounding country there is much pasturage; the soldiers agreed that all their horses could be maintained there. These Indians raise much squash, melons, maize, and beans; they supplied rations of all these things to our people and bartered some also for beads which the Commander had given his soldiers. A good supply of provisions was thus obtained. None of the expedition could stop praising this land. I too stayed here on the 8th.

Dec. 9 *30th day*   4
Saying good-bye to the Commander, Father Font, and all the others, I left with my interpreters, accompanied by several Cajuenches and a Yuma Indian who lives among them, and travelled four leagues southwest, which brought me to the rancherías called La Merced and inhabited by Cajuenches. In this land there is a sufficiency of fodder and many plantings of squash, watermelons, maize, and beans; I missed only wheat. I gave them tobacco and beads and through the Yumas who live among them, and my interpreters, I spoke to them of God and His mysteries and explained the paintings

[16]

on the canvas. They showed great joy at everything, as also at seeing me, for they were already acquainted with me and knew that I was with the Yumas. The Cajuenche language is very different from Yuma, so my interpreters were not of much use to me. However, I resorted to having my Indians talk with the Yumas, and the Yumas with the Cajuenches, who as they are neighbouring nations understand each other well. I was astonished to see in this land such an abundance of seed crops, for when I was here in the year '71 they were very sparse. When I asked why, they told me they used to do much sowing but little reaping because the Yumas, who were their enemies, would come down at harvest time, kill them, and destroy their fields. Now that they were their friends they would have much to eat. I saw at this place about three hundred souls.

Dec. 10   *31st day*   *1 ½*
Continuing a league and a half southwest, from one ranchería to another, I saw the same abundance of provisions, and the Indians gave me the same explanation: they had kept the peace which at my intervention they had made at the time of my other visit to their land. This was why they now showed me such affection and were so generous with gifts; it was astonishing to see the abundance of watermelons, corn tortillas, muskmelons, various gruels, and fish that they gave me.

Dec. 11   *32nd day*   *1*
This day I travelled one league southwest. I took an observation at the place I came to and found it to be at 32° 25′. Very many people gathered here today, among them an Indian of the Cucapá nation, which occupies a large area along the Laguna de San Mateo[9] as far as to the mountains, to the Colorado River, and to the river's mouth. This nation is an enemy of the Jalliquamais, or Quiquimás; also of the Quemeyás, who live in the mountains, and of the Cajuenches. I greeted the Cucapá Indian warmly and gave him presents. He told me that in his land they were already aware that I was travelling in those regions, and that was why he had come to see me on behalf of

9. Apparently a channel of the Colorado River; see the entry for December 18. The Laguna de Santa Eulalia mentioned on December 6 and 7 may also have been, at one time, an overflow channel.

[17]

his nation. With him was an old woman. I told them both to give their people my greetings and to say that I would go there within three days. I showed them my crucifix, breviary, and compass so they might see I was the same man that had been in their country some years before. They soon took their leave. The Cajuenches continued showing their joy with big dances and much shouting. Throughout this league's extent I saw many sown fields.

Dec. 12   *33rd day*   *2*

A large crowd gathered in the ranchería where I had slept, mostly men, who performed an extravagant dance. So great was the crush of people upon me whenever I left my shelter that I was obliged to stay inside it. At noon I heard loud howls, shouts, and running-around. Going outside, I learned what was the matter. A Cajuenche Indian had been stabbed with a spear by a Jalliquamai and the flint, entering through his shoulder, had gone in near his heart. As a piece of the spearhead was still in him, they decided to remove it from the front, thus making him suffer a second time. The medicine man at once began his office of running, huffing, and whirling about. I endeavoured to pacify them, for they wanted to kill a young man whom they brought before me. When I became aware of their intention I told them they should give it up, but when he was on his way to his ranchería others came out to defend him, and so a free-for-all fight began. The old men would launch arrows and the young men would run in to catch those let fly by their opponents. There were no further casualties except that one man was beaten with a club. I expostulated with the captain of the ranchería because they had so little common sense as to start fighting when I had come to establish peace among them. He answered me that what was done could not be undone, but there would be no more. The interpreters I had with me, having seen what happened, said they would not go with me to the Cucapás; and the Indians added to their fears by asserting that those downriver would do the same to us if we should go to their lands, and refused us guides for the way through. And not only were the interpreters daunted, but also those others who were travelling with me, wherefore they made me leave hurriedly, fearful that some might come at night to stab us, or to steal our

PIMA WOMEN, AND YUMAS
From drawings by Arthur Schott *reproduced as chromolithographs in 1857*

PIMA WOMEN, AND YUMAS
From drawings by Arthur Schott *reproduced as chromolithographs in 1857*

PIMA WOMEN

YUMAS

horses. I yielded about leaving, first instructing in the Faith as best I could the man with the stab wound, who gladly received Holy Baptism.

At this ranchería the Cajuenche nation ends. I left accompanied by many Jalliquamais and, going about two leagues east, arrived at one of that people's rancherías, of about two hundred souls. In this land there is little pasturage, but they have a great supply of provisions and are very generous. I noticed also that the Indians of this nation are more cleanly than the Yumas and Cajuenches, and as they do not get so dirty the women appeared half white. They all received me with great pleasure and feasted me splendidly. I spoke to them as best I could about God. They gave me to understand that they acquiesced in what I was telling them, and upon seeing the paintings they showed that they felt about them as the Cajuenches did. I was not able to explain myself so well to these Jalliquamais, because although their language seems to be the same as that of the Cajuenches the difference is marked. On account of the happenings at the other ranchería I decided to cross the Colorado and visit the Cucapá nation. I started the next day.

Dec. 13   *34th day*   *1 ½*

I left going east but could not continue in that direction as I was told that neither east nor south were there any people; that those I had seen on the earlier occasion had gone over to the other side of the river because of their enemies. I changed direction from east to northeast and, having gone a league and a half, stopped at a ranchería of Jalliquamais which had perhaps two hundred souls. In these rancherías the Jalliquamais live after the manner of a village, as the Cajuenches do, the better to defend themselves when they fight their enemies. They all received me well, for these Jalliquamais lived on the other side of the river in the year '71, in the rancherías to which I had then given the name of Santa Rosa. Seeing that my idea of crossing the river had come to nothing, I decided to go back to the ranchería nearest the Cajuenches.

Dec. 14   I returned to the ranchería from which I left on the 13th.

[19]

Dec. 15 *35th day*

I went two leagues west and stopped near the ranchería of the wounded Indian whom I had baptized as I have related above. He had died that night. The ranchería was made up of some two hundred Jalliquamais and Cajuenches. I stayed here both this day and the next because it was very cold. They treated me well.

Dec. 17 *36th day*

Travelling three leagues south-southeast, I came to the Laguna de San Mateo, which I crossed in the arms of the Cajuenches who were accompanying me. Putting me down on the other side, they took their leave because here their territory ends and that of the Cucapás, with whom they are enemies, begins. I kept on my way; continuing four leagues in the same direction, I reached the sown fields of the Cucapás which were deserted and ruined because, not long before, Yumas, Cajuenches, and Jalliquamais had fought the Cucapás there. I spent the night at this place and feasted on some most delicious watermelons. Pasturage abounds in all these parts.

Dec. 18 When I was preparing to go on my way I saw some Indians travelling in the upriver direction. I called to them and they came with cheerful shouts as is their custom. They were Cucapás who said they had come looking for me. Once before they had come out for the same purpose; a message had reached them that within three days I should come to visit them and therefore all the people were expecting me. At this place fodder is plentiful, there is much common reed-grass and reed-mace; and there are fine tablelands with a very pleasing outlook, the river being about three leagues away. I consider this place very suitable for a mission since it need fear no floods. I am convinced that at the time of freshets this Laguna de San Mateo, which now stretches over some leagues, becomes a great arm of the river; but its bed is deep and so the tablelands here can escape flooding.

I got on my horse and, having gone four leagues south-southeast, leaving on my right the Sierra de San Gerónimo, three leagues away, I stopped at a ranchería of the Cucapás. Throughout the four leagues' distance were the rancherías and crops of these Indians, who were so numerous that although I began by giving presents to all, I had to limit them to women only.

I had stopped already, but the Indian Sebastián, who was the only one with me (the other two Indians had stayed, full of misgivings, with the Cajuenches), begged me not to stop here because fodder was scarce and the water was in a place where the animals could not drink. In order for us to get both, an old Indian who seemed an important one offered himself, saying that he would take me to his dwelling-place. We set out for it, going three leagues southeast, and passed two rancherías on the way. It was already nightfall when I arrived at the old man's place, where a large number of people gathered, including an old woman who understood the Yuma language well. Through this old woman and the Indian Sebastián, who knows a little Yuma, I spoke to them about the peace. Now that all the upriver nations were friends, I said, they would not come downriver to harm them, and they should no longer go upriver to fight. This proposal suited them well because, they said, the wars held them back and forced them to live where there was little water and no firewood. The old woman, however, seemed unwilling to believe what I said to her. I asked her about two small children whom I had baptized when I was in their country in the year '71 and she began to weep, saying: "Both are dead. Don't you remember, I am the mother of one of them?" I gave presents to all and consoled the old woman, telling her that her son was now in Heaven.

As all my baggage had been left with the interpreters who stayed with the Cajuenches, I was not able to show them the painting of the Virgin, though they implored me to do so because they had been told of it by those who saw it at the other rancherías and so knew that I carried it. I spoke to them of God and showed them the crucifix, which they all kissed. They fingered my breviary and begged me to show them its pictures, for they had also been told that it had five or six and so they were not content with seeing just one. The compass, too, had to go from hand to hand, notwithstanding they had seen it at the time of my earlier journey.

I asked about the sea and about the Indians who had carried me across the river in the year '71. They answered that both sea and Indians were near.

In the morning I went three leagues south-southeast and southwest, visiting a number of rancherías made up of people from that region and from the mountains. In the ranchería visited last they urged me vehemently to stay, but I did not because the Indian Sebastián told me that the place had only swamp reeds and standing water. Although the Indians told me that downriver there was neither pasturage nor sweet water, paying no attention I went my way and soon came to wide sandy flats without fodder and with water only in some stagnant pools; it was brackish. I stopped here and took an observation, finding the latitude to be 32° 17′. Then I continued southward again, with occasional deviations to the southwest and southeast because of the flats. The Indians who had come with me that morning from the last ranchería warned me that I would find no more sweet water, nor fodder, because the sea when it rose covered all that land; and as Sebastián reminded me that our beasts had not drunk all day I resolved to turn back to the nearest ranchería so that I could make a more leisurely start the next day. I arrived that night at the rancherías which I have come to believe are the last down the river, namely, those I had called on my previous journey the Rancherías de las Llagas. There I found the Indians who in the year ’71 took me across the Colorado, To them, and to me too, it was a great comfort. In order to arrive at this ranchería I had come four leagues northeast from where I had taken the observation.

Dec. 20 I stopped at this ranchería, distributing gifts to the Indians. As best I could, I talked to them about God and about their having priests there. They were most grateful and pleased. I took an observation and found the latitude to be 32° 18′.

I travelled over a very wide treeless and grassless flat for five leagues to the southwest, with a few shifts to the southeast and south. I came to the water that was of the sea. Although salty, it had mixed here with the Colorado River and was not so bitter as that of the sea proper. Its waves were high and it stretched northeast as well as south as far as one could see. East and west it extended a little more than a league. By all these signs I knew that I was at the mouth of the

Colorado River, but to make more certain I went a league further down and had the Indian fetch water; it was too salt to drink. I went back and stopped where I had first tested. Here I noticed that at nightfall the currents which in the morning flowed northeast now turned southwest and already were exposing to view a low island. A great murmur of flowing water could be heard, making me think that the river discharged through two mouths not far from each other, but the next day I saw that there was only one. All night I heard the great murmur of waters.

Dec. 22 Going back to where I had been the evening before, I found the whole shore dry except that a little water was left in a deep channel. I dropped a log in to see if it would move, but it stayed still. In the night the water had come by the tideways more than thirty paces further up than where I was on the 21st. The murmur could no longer be heard. The water in this channel and in the other tidepools was salt, though not so much so as that of the sea; from which I gather that on the 21st I arrived here at high water or when the tide was beginning to ebb and that this is certainly the mouth of the Colorado River. The murmur I heard at night was undoubtedly that of the second tide.

I returned to the Rancherías de las Llagas, where the Indians told me, and I noticed it too, that the tide reached these rancherías because the shoreland was very flat. When the Colorado River rises, these waters extend to the Sierra de Santa Bárbara, which is a branch, toward the southeast, of the Sierra Madre of California. It ends at these shores and leaves open a great valley as far as the Sierra de San Gerónimo, which ends where I spent the night of the 18th. From this I gather that at the time of the great floods of the river the water probably rises along this shore between the Sierra de Santa Bárbara and the Sierra de San Gerónimo as far as the place where the first expedition came upon a great number of fish that were beached or on dry land, as is mentioned in its travel record.

Behind the Sierra de Santa Bárbara I saw another and greater mountain range which begins in the Sierra Madre of California and ends on the seacoast; I called it the Sierra de la Natividad. Behind these two mountain ranges is another higher still, which, also issuing

[23]

from the Sierra Madre, ends on the shore at a point where there is an opening or bay through which, the Indians told me, the waters meet; I called it the Sierra de San Pedro. Looking to the east I could see a high, short mountain range that seemed to me to be the Sierra Prieta, which, as I wrote in the year '71, lies toward the west of Sonoitac.

From all the foregoing I am convinced that when the Colorado River is not in flood one can cross here to go to the missions of Lower California, since many of the mountain Indians who have come here to eat the natural products of this land have asked me if I was going to visit the priests of Lower California or those of San Diego. These heathen who come down to the river from the mountains are a distinctly different nation: very poor, very ugly, and in poor health, and they go around in a very filthy state because of the large amount of mescal they eat. Their language is totally different from that of the river peoples.

They were very agreeable to me and in order to amuse me brought a little girl about ten years old, who, covering only the absolute minimum, threw her right leg over her left shoulder, took a stick in her hand, and in this fashion danced, hopped, and ran about, afterward repeating with the left leg. This brought great shouts of laughter from the mountain Indians and the Cucapás of the ranchería where I was staying. A short machete that my Indian had was stolen, and the river Indians were so much put out about it that if I had not calmed them down they would have destroyed the ranchería to which the little thief belonged.

One could tell that these poor folk had never seen domesticated animals, especially mules, for Sebastián told me that they greeted ours as if they were persons; at any rate, on two or three different nights they compassionately removed the mules' hobbles and took them to another ranchería to eat squash. On another day the jack mule got stuck in the mud. When the Indians saw that he couldn't free himself they all ran to help him, took him out in their arms, and carried him to the fire to get warm.

Dec. 23   *39th day*   *4½*
We set out eastward and passed a watering-place, and, having gone half a league, came to a ranchería of some two hundred souls, and

another, not far off, that seemed to be of mountain people. I gave them presents. Then, going northwest and north four leagues more, we came out near the river facing some high knolls on the other side to which in the year '71 I had given the name of Buena Vista. I told the Indians that here were to be placed the priest's house and those of the Spaniards. They were very happy at this news, and they told me that they would carry the logs for building the priest's house. This site, which I saw from the knolls, is one of the best anywhere along the Colorado River for the founding of a mission; it is a broad tableland, very high near the river, with a good amount of pasturage on the downstream side and not far away a swampy pool with water.

The Indians asked me when we should be going on, for they fear those further upriver. From here they turned back to their rancherías and I went on upstream, taking a good look at the country as far as the territory of the Yumas. I calculated the number of the Cucapá nation to be about three thousand; of the Jalliquamai, about two thousand; and of the Cajuenche, about three thousand. Of the mountain people I could make no estimate, as I saw only those who came down to the river; but those here say that, as compared with them, the mountain people are few.

It took me the rest of the month and until January 3 to reach the territory of the Yumas, where I had left my companion Father Tomás.

Jan. 3
1776
I arrived at night at the Puerto de la Concepción,[10] where I was happy to find my well-beloved companion in good health and much pleased with the Yumas. He told me that while I was away they had waited upon him and met his needs unsparingly; they had made tortillas for him to eat as if he were in his Mission. I gave thanks to God when I heard them chant some divine praises which the Father had taught them and when I saw that many of them came to hear Mass. In all this the foremost was Captain Palma, who, although a heathen, put many Christians to shame by the reverence with which he followed the Mass, imitating the Catholics in crossing himself, beating his breast, and other signs of devotion. From this it struck my companion and me that he and all his Yumas are quite ready to receive the Faith and that in a short time this entire nation may be added to the Church. I asked Palma if he had any knowledge of God before coming into contact with the Fathers, to which he answered yes, but not so clearly as now. With regard to what happens to souls, he held to the same fantasies as are related of the Opas. He told me that we do not feel the death of our relatives as they the death of theirs; for he had seen burials of Spaniards (this captain has been several times at the Presidio of Altar; also in Horcasitas,[11] when he went to visit Governor Crespo to ask that priests and Spaniards should come to his country) and had noticed that our people did not lament as his people do. The remaining details about this nation, and about others that I have seen, I shall relate in my "Reflections" upon this record.

While I was here the Cocomaricopas and Jalcheduns came, to whom, as my interpreter explained to me, Captain Palma spoke as follows: "We now are brothers who formerly were enemies. This benefit has come to us through the Fathers and the Spaniards, and

---

10. See Maj. W. H. Emory's *Notes of a ... Reconnaissance ... Made in 1846-7*, p. 95: "The Gila comes into [the Colorado] nearly at right angles, and the point of junction, strangely chosen, is the hard butte through which with their united force they cut a cañon, and then flow off due magnetic west.... The walls of the cañon are vertical and about 50 feet high, and 1,000 feet long." This is the Puerto de la Concepción.

11. Horcasitas, a major Spanish settlement in Sonora province, had as a *villa* (as it is called in the manuscript) a municipal form of government with a large measure of autonomy. Francisco Antonio Crespo was the governor of Sonora, 1774-1777.

for that reason I have cast aside my weapons; don't think it is from fear. You must already be aware that I have many men and that the Cajuenches, Quemeyás, Yavipais, and Jamajabs are now my friends. You, Jalcheduns, have said to me that you are not resolute in the peace we have made. Take up your weapons if you will; I am able, with the Spaniards, to punish you. Tell me, who are we to stand against the soldiers? They already control the road entirely, for you know there are Spaniards on the seacoast and near Moqui." From this speech it can be seen that the Indians are not so stupid as some think; and by the special providence of God they fear even where there is little to be afraid of.

At this time I baptized seven persons who were near death.

As the Danzarines, who live in the Puerto de San Carlos mountain range and toward the north, saw that their friends the Jalcheduns had now made peace with the Yumas, they came down, knowing that we were there, and made their peace with them also. These Indians, whom on the earlier expedition we had called Danzarines because of their ridiculous motions when they talk, are known to the nations on the river by the name of Jequiches.

As a sign of friendship the Cajuenches invited Captain Palma and his friends to come down to visit their lands and eat squash.

A Quemeyá Indian arrived and related, as the message was reported to us, that two or three nations had joined together to fight the Spaniards of the seacoast; that already they had killed one priest and burned his house, but had done nothing to the Spaniards who had passed through Yuma territory because they knew them to be their friends; that if those Spaniards should join with the ones of the coast, and together they should make war on the Indians, then the Indians would defend themselves and strip the Spaniards of all that they had. The Quemeyá Indian said he was bringing this message on behalf of his nation because the Quemeyás knew the Indians here to be old friends; his nation did not ask these Indians to take up arms, but to be neutral if there should be war. As we were always hearing all sorts of stories from the Indians, we did not at the time give much weight to this news; but it turned out to be true.[12] It is

---

12. The Indian outbreak at San Diego had occurred on November 4-5 preceding.

easy to see how important it is for us to have on our side the nations of the river, so that we can not only go through to our Monterey establishments, but also provide for their subsistence, a matter I shall deal with in my "Reflections."

Besides the Jalcheduns who were continually visiting us, there came to this place nine Indians of the nation called Tejua Yavipais, known to us as Apaches. These are old friends of the Yumas, who on that account got up a great feast; they came, as is their custom every year, to eat of the earth's abundance. They come in winter because the way is then good; it is a five days' journey over broken country. These Tejua Yavipais danced while we ate. Afterward we showed them the pictures and all the rest, and they expressed much pleasure. On the next day they heard Mass just as attentively as Captain Palma.

There was a Yuma who understood the Apaches' language, and through him I asked them how they lived; how they maintained themselves; what friends they had; and if they ever went to the land of the Spaniards, or the latter to their land. They answered that they lived scattered over their country; that they subsisted by hunting, though they also raised a little maize and squash; that their old friends were the Yumas, Jamajabs, and Yavipais of the east; that they were enemies of the Spaniards, who had never come to their land, nor had they gone to ours; that they were also enemies of the Yavipais of the north, the Hopis, the Cocomaricopas, and the Gileños, but since, according to what they had heard, all were making peace they too would make peace with all; that they had heard that the Yavipais of the east, their friends, were very apprehensive because many Spaniards were entering their lands.

I said to them that if they should all gather in one good place and present their children to be baptized I would come to see them and they would have peace with all their enemies; then the Fathers and the Spaniards would come to live on the Gila and Colorado rivers and all the nations would be friends and everything would be all right. The Apaches answered that on returning to their land they would assemble the people and tell them everything that Captain Palma and I had proposed. I explained to them that the Spaniards did no harm to good people and that if the bad stopped being bad there would be no more fighting.

These Apaches and the Cocomaricopas advised me that the Gila River was beginning to rise and that this year it would bring down much water, which required our moving our hut from Captain Palma's place to the Puerto de la Concepción. This was done by my companion aided by the interpreters and some Yumas; but let it not therefore be thought that in future the heathen must have to build priest's house and church, for we know the ill results that may follow. These first buildings must be put up by the hands of Spaniards or of the soldiers themselves, with at least one room of adobe bricks for storing the most necessary things brought along.

On one of the days I was here, I went down to the Puerto de San Pablo to have a better look for a mission site. I found one between the mountains and the sands of the shore, among some high knolls that are beyond the Puerto near a channel through which water runs when the river is high and when no waterholes can be dug; and, moreover, the bank of the river can be scooped away so that the channel will have running water the year round. This site has pasturage enough. I consider it most suitable for founding a mission.

The Jalcheduns came repeatedly to see me, urging me to go to their land. I would have complied with pleasure on condition that they take me to the country of the Jamajabs, but this they objected to, from fear of them, and they answered no, that they would only take me through their land and afterward return me to the Yumas. Seeing how strong the objection was, I decided to go first to the Jamajabs with an Indian of that nation who was there.

Feb. 14   *40th day of journey*   *Leagues travelled 4½*
Having taken leave of my companion, I left the Puerto de la Concepción, accompanied by Sebastián, two interpreters, and the Jamajab Indian. With them I travelled four and a half leagues northwest.

Feb. 15   *41st day*   *2*
I went on two leagues in the same direction.

Feb. 16   *42nd day*   *2*
I went on two leagues west-northwest, crossing the San Pablo

[29]

mountain range through a pass at the side of which I found rain-water in a gully with some vegetation. My old interpreter, who knew something about mining, said the ground there must have plenty of gold in it because iron oxide was much in evidence. The land lacks herbage. I called its watering-place the Aguaje de San Marcelo.

Feb. 17 43rd day 1

I travelled a league northwest.

Feb. 18 44th day 4

Going four leagues northwest, I caught a distant glimpse of the Cabeza del Gigante to the east, and I made out also the extensive dune country with the surroundings of San Sebastián. I passed near the Peñon de la Campana, which from here looks quite different.[13]

Feb. 19 45th day 8

Having gone eight leagues north with short shifts north-northeast, I crossed by a very good pass the mountain range which lies to the north of the dune country. The watering-place where I stopped for the night consists of several pools right down in the floor of a ravine, from which the animals can drink easily. There is plenty of herbage. I called this place San José. It is a day's journey from here to the river eastward, and another to the territory of the Jequiches, where they tell me there are many pools of water, though it is somewhat brackish. I infer from the foregoing that this is a better route than that followed by the expedition.

Feb. 20

I rested at this place, San José, which I found to be at latitude 33° 18′. There is a mountain range, running west to east, which joins that of California.

Feb. 21 46th day 3½ [? 2½]

Having travelled half a league north-northwest and two leagues east-northeast, I crossed the mountains and came to a valley where I found some eighty Jamajabs who were on their way down to the

---

13. The Cabeza del Gigante ('Giant's Head') is now called Castle Dome. The small ranchería and brackish watering-place of San Sebastián was just below the Salton Sea, where there is still an extensive sand-dune region. The Peñon de la Campana ('Bell Rock'), later known as Chimney Rock, is now on the maps as Picacho Peak.

Yumas on account of the news which I have recounted. I treated them kindly and gave them food because they were very hungry. As I spoke to them about the peace between the Yumas and the Jalcheduns, they showed me two Jalchedun girls whom they had as captives. I asked for them very insistently, and finally, after overcoming several difficulties, I succeeded; they gave them to me in exchange for a bad horse and some other gifts of small value. They continued on their way except the captain with a few others, who stayed with me that night, sending their animals to San José to drink.

Feb. 22   *47th day*   6
I went on four leagues north-northwest and two east-northeast, making a circuit because the Jamajabs told me that the laden mules could not go straight up.

Feb. 23   *48th day*   6
Travelling two leagues east-northeast and four north, I climbed a mountain range that comes from the west; I called it the Sierra de Santa Margarita. Here I found the Colorado River alongside. Crossing a valley, I came to a watering-place in the ravine of another mountain range coming from the west. I made this circuit (which is not necessary) because the Jamajabs were at war with the Jalcheduns.

Feb. 24   *49th day*   1 ½
I took an observation and found the place to be at 33° 25′. In the afternoon I went a league and a half westward, with some deviations because the way through the mountains was poor.

Feb. 25   *50th day*   6
I crossed the mountain range through a good pass to the northwest, and going west-northwest I came to the pools of Tesquien three leagues further on. These pools are well supplied and are very convenient for watering the animals. This place, which is a day's journey from the river, makes it possible to travel from the land of the Jalcheduns to that of the Jenigueches, who are the people of the Santa Anna River. In the afternoon I travelled three leagues north-northwest across a tiring stretch of sand.

I decided to send the Jalchedun girls back to their home with my old interpreter, who was to give many messages on my behalf and say that as they [the Jalcheduns] were now friends of the Jamajabs all the old hostilities were ended. I told my interpreter to go on up to the Jamajabs' country and wait for me there. The Jamajab captain made a great speech to the Jalchedun girls and to the interpreter for the Jalcheduns, and as a sign of true peace broke his bow and threw away his arrows.

This day I went eight leagues north-northeast and north and crossed a mountain range running northwest. On my way down I stopped at some little springs which I named after the Holy Angel. Here I met forty of the Chemevet nation. Six of them came down, fleet as deer, as soon as we called them. All gave me very good mescal. Their dress consists of Apache footgear, a garment of deer-hide, and a white cap resembling a skullcap with a bunch of very quaint feathers which certain birds have on their heads as a crest. I judge these Indians to be the best runners of any I have seen.

This nation occupies a bit of land, very short of water, between the territory of the Beñemés and that of the Jamajabs, which then continues along the northern bank of the Colorado River to the land of the Yuta nation, of whom they gave much information, as also of the Comanches. They are enemies of the latter and of the Hopis, and friends of the Yutas. They said that their nation reaches as far as another river that flows north of the Colorado, and that there they sow crops. They also are on friendly terms with the Tejua Apaches. Their language is different from those of all the river nations. They are close friends of the Jamajabs, and when these cast aside their weapons they do so too. They make baskets[14] very similar to those of the [Santa Barbara] Channel [Indians]. In the various regions where they live, they have different names; they are called Cajuala Sevinta, Cajuala Chemevet, or Chemeguagua. Toward me they behaved very well. They are not given to thieving, nor are they restless. They have much good sense. Besides their weapons they all carry a curved stick [for use in hunting small game].

---

14. The manuscript reads *cueritas* by error for *coritas;* the baskets are correctly mentioned as *coritas* in the entry for March 1.

Feb. 27 *52nd day*   6

I took an observation at this place, [the springs of] the Holy Angel, and found it to be at 34° 31′. Afterward I went on six leagues to the northeast and northwest, the longer stretch being the former, and then I halted though there was no water, only fodder.

Feb. 28 *53rd day*   7

I went on seven leagues north-northeast and, having crossed a mountain range [the Mojave] running northwest and ending at the Colorado River, I reached the territory of the Jamajab nation. To their rancherías, which were on the other side of the river, I gave the name La Pasión. I did not cross the river, but the people came to see me because the captain who was travelling with me went ahead to give them notice of my coming. All who crossed over that day stayed with me, and so to my satisfaction I was able to speak with them on all matters of interest. They gave approval to everything: I should ask permission and stay to baptize them, for they were sure that things would then go well.

I can say in all truth that these Indians are superior in many things to the Yumas and the rest of the Colorado River nations. They are less troublesome, and they are not thievish. They show spirit, and are very obliging; nowhere have I been better taken care of.

I showed them the painting of the Virgin, which pleased them very much; of the Damned Man they said that he was very bad. I was the first Spaniard to enter their land, at which they rejoiced greatly on account of their desire to know us. They had heard said that we were brave, and they showed extraordinary pleasure at being friends of so valiant a people.

Feb. 29 I remained here because there came from time to time so very many. Among them were three captains, one of whom was the foremost of the nation; without him nothing was decided. He came so that I might tell him what was to be done, and he said to me that I would know who he was [referring to his station] when he should have done what I had told him, for his heart was good; he would be baptized and would marry one wife; and he added other good things. This captain is the most important of all and lives in the center of their territory.

[33]

These people are very healthy and robust. The women are the most attractive of any along the river. They wear skirts of the same material and design as those of the Yuma women. The men go stark naked; in so cold a land it excites pity. They say they are very hardy, especially in bearing hunger and thirst, and I found this to be so. It is evident that this nation is on the increase, for it abounds in young people and children while the contrary is to be noticed in the other nations of the river. I was visited by some two thousand persons. Common here are blankets made of woven [strips of] rabbit fur, and of otter which they get from the west and northwest since they are on very friendly terms with the people who live there. They have also been on close terms with the Yumas; their languages are unlike, but from dealing back and forth they understand each other well enough. They speak forcibly and haughtily. I have never heard any Indian speak with more self-confidence than the captain I have mentioned. Their enemies are: on the northeast, the Cuercomache Yavipais; on the east, the Jaguallapais; on the south, the Jalcheduns. When making speeches they give their thighs hard slaps.

I laid before them my desires to visit the Fathers living near the sea; they gave assent and offered to accompany me, for they had heard of them and knew the way. As I was now short of supplies, I decided to leave at once and told them that on my return we should see each other at leisure. I left some of my baggage. The interpreter whom I had sent to the Jalcheduns with the Indian girls that I had ransomed had not returned, so with Sebastián and the Jamajabs for company I left this place.

Mar. 1   *54th day*   *3*
I travelled three leagues northwest accompanied by the principal captain of the Jamajabs, and keeping away from the growing wheat I came to the rancherías to which I gave the name Santa Isabel, where was the captain's dwelling.

Mar. 2   I stopped at the captain's request for the satisfaction of those who wished to see me. This day there visited me another captain with his people, and two Indians of the Chemevet nation.

Mar. 3 *55th day* **3**

I went northwest, with occasional turns west-northwest, three leagues. I took an observation at this place (the rancherías here I called San Pedro de los Jamajabs) and found the latitude to be 35° 01'. Here and at other places further down there are good tablelands for building missions; although they are near the river, they are free from flooding.

Mar. 4 *56th day* **2½**

I set out to the southwest, accompanied by three Jamajab Indians and Sebastián. After two and a half leagues I arrived at some water-holes which I named the Pozos de San Casimiro. There was some pasturage.

Mar. 5 *57th day* **8**

Setting out northwest, I went eight leagues west by a quarter west-southwest through flat and grass-covered country and halted where there were holes with excellent water, but it was not very plentiful; Sebastián said that watering might be possible in two shifts.

Mar. 6 *58th day* **5**

I went five leagues west and three west-southwest through flat and grassy country and came to a mountain range [the Providence] with small pines; I called it the Sierra de Santa Coleta. The watering-place has little yield and is high up. Pasturage is ample and of good quality. Here I met four Indians who had come from Santa Clara to traffic in shell beads. They were carrying no food supply, nor even bows for hunting. Noticing my astonishment at this, where there is nothing to eat, they said, "We Jamajabs can withstand hunger and thirst for as long as four days," giving me to understand that they were hardy men.

Mar. 7 *59th day* **4**

In the afternoon I crossed the mountain range by a good pass and entered a small valley with sandy knolls at its sides; I called it the Cañada de Santo Tomás. Having travelled four leagues west-north-west (although I would have done better to follow the valley, as it had the firmest ground), I halted. At my stopping-place there was herbage but no water.

[35]

Mar. 8   *60th day*   *6*

Six leagues to the west-southwest I came to some waterholes with an abundant supply; I named them after San Juan de Dios. Pasturage was sufficient. Here begins the territory of the Beñemé nation.

Mar. 9   *61st day*   *5*

I went on five leagues and came to a pass in the mountains; I gave it the name Pinta because of the veins of various colors that are in it. I found a stream-bed with rather brackish water [the Mojave River] and named it the Arroyo de los Mártires. There was good pasturage.

Mar. 10   *62nd day*   *6*

I continued six leagues west-southwest and stopped in the same stream-bed, where there are cottonwoods, pools of water, and much herbage.

Mar. 11   *63rd day*   *1*

Going on another league in the same direction, I came to some poor rancherías; they had nothing to eat but the roots of rushes. The inhabitants numbered about twenty-five. I gave them of what little I had, and they gave me of their roots, which my Jamajab companions swallowed with repugnance. The Indians showed disappointment at not being able to go hunting to get me food, but it was rainy and very cold and they were stark naked.

Here are found wild grapes, much pasturage, and mesquites including the screwbean. This nation is the same as that of San Gabriel, Santa Clara, and San José. They have some baskets like those of the [Santa Barbara] Channel [Indians], blankets of otter and rabbit, and some very unusual nets which they make from the wild hemp that grows here. The men are effeminate, and the women rather dirty like those of the mountains; but they are all very peaceable and not at all troublesome. They listened attentively to what I told them of God.

Mar. 12   *64th day*   *2*

Having gone two leagues in the same direction, I stopped at a deserted ranchería on the same watercourse. The rain and cold continued; also our hunger, because there was not so much as rush roots; and as the inhabited rancherías were a long distance away I decided to have a horse killed to relieve our necessity. Not even the blood was wasted, and rationing was necessary until we got to other rancherías. The cold was so severe that one of the Jamajab Indians accompanying me started back. To one of the two who stayed on I gave a blanket to keep him warm, and to the other a woollen shirt. With the slaughtering of the horse there was much to eat, and they did not want to leave for three days.

Mar. 15   *65th day*   *3 ½*
I moved on two leagues west-southwest and one and a half leagues northwest and halted on the same watercourse. Pasturage is plentiful.

Mar. 16   *66th day*   *4*
I went two leagues west-northwest, left the watercourse, and turned southwest. There I came to it again and followed it, going southward until I had completed four leagues. The herbage is good, and there are large cottonwoods, and cranes and crows like those of San Gabriel.

Mar. 17   I was there the whole day because on crossing the stream the mule got stuck and everything got wet. I sent a Jamajab and Sebastián to look for inhabited rancherías. This place is at 34° 37′. There came to it five Jamajab Indians who had just returned from trading at San Gabriel, well pleased at their treatment by the Fathers, who had given them maize. These Indians imitated the bleating of the [mission's] calves.

Mar. 18   *67th day*   *5*
Sebastián returned praising the hospitality he had received. I mounted and rode five leagues southwest up this watercourse to a ranchería of forty souls, of the same Beñemé nation. Because I had come below 35° [of latitude] I urged the Indians to take me toward the west, but they refused, saying they knew no other route. Here I was treated to hares, rabbits, and plenty of acorn gruel, with which we relieved our hunger.

Mar. 19   *68th day*   *1*
I went one league south-southwest and reached the dwelling of the

captain of these rancherías. He gave me a string of white seashells that was about two yards long. His wife sprinkled me with acorns and threw the basket, which is a sign of marked attention. Then she brought out some seashells and sprinkled me with them as if she were tossing flowers. Then his second wife came and expressed her sentiments with the same attentions. I responded in the best way I could, astonished that among such rustic people there should be so expressive a show of feeling as their pouring out the shells that are their greatest treasure.

Mar. 20   *69th day*   7½
I travelled two and a half leagues east and southeast following the watercourse and came to a pass through which the stream flows; the position was 34° 18′. I continued in the afternoon and having gone five leagues south and southwest I arrived at a ranchería of perhaps seventy souls where the inhabitants received me with high spirits, some howling like wolves and others orating at the top of their voices. There were two captains. They and all the other men gave me seashells and the women made the same display of feeling as those at the ranchería last visited, tossing acorns even to the mules.

Mar. 21   *70th day*   3
Striking out to the southwest from the stream and travelling two leagues, I crossed a ravine and some low hills, coming to a ranchería of five huts, and kept on south through a valley with many trees, pasturage, and water. In it there are many cottonwoods, alders, oaks, very tall conifers, and sightly junipers. A league further on I came to another ranchería of about eighty souls, which I called San Benito. I was joyfully received and treated to a shower of acorns.

Mar. 22   *71st day*   6
After three leagues I crossed the [San Bernardino] mountain range south-southwest. The trees mentioned yesterday reach to its top, whence the Ocean is in view, the Santa Anna River, and the San José Valley. On the downslope of the range there are few trees. At its foot I found a ranchería where they received me very gladly. I continued west-southwest and west, and having gone three leagues along the slope of the range I stopped in the Arroyo de los Alisos.

[38]

Mar. 23 *72nd day* *10½*

I travelled half a league west-southwest and a league south, at the urging of some Indians whom I met and who made me go to their ranchería, where we ate. After going another league west-southwest, I struck the path of the expedition. I followed it rapidly, going eight leagues northwest and west-northwest, well into the night, when I halted.

Mar. 24 *73rd day* *2*

Two leagues to the west-northwest brought me to San Gabriel Mission, where I was most kindly received by the Fathers. It made me very happy to see the improvement in this mission, both spiritual and temporal, since my former visit.

My principal object on leaving the Jamajabs' country was to go straight to San Luis [Obispo] Mission, or further north, to make communication easier between the Sonora and Moqui provinces and Monterey (which is what His Excellency the Viceroy seeks); but not having succeeded in doing so because my Indian companions had refused to go with me, I decided to go from San Gabriel up to San Luis over the Camino Real[15] and then, striking eastward, to examine what reed marshes there are to the east of San Luis; and, continuing in the same direction, to return to the Jamajabs' country. For this journey I asked the corporal at San Gabriel for an escort and supplies, but he refused me. I appealed to Commander Rivera,[16] who at the time was in San Diego, and he also, in writing, flatly refused my request. A few days after I received his reply, he arrived in San Gabriel and I set forth to him that matters were not impracticable as he had written, since many of the expedition's animals were there and that the Fathers, on his order, would give me supplies; also, since he was on his way to Monterey, I could go in his company past the [Santa Barbara] Channel, the most dangerous region,[17] after

15. The 'highway', no more than a horse trail, that linked the few missions then established in Upper California.

16. Fernando Xavier de Rivera y Moncada, military governor of Upper California. He had a prickly side to his character, as the record of his career shows; see, e.g., H. H. Bancroft, *History of California*, Vol. I.

17. By this route Father Garcés would have reached San Luis Obispo Mission and, further on, that of San Carlos Borromeo, near Monterey. Later in this same year (1776) almost all the mission buildings at San Luis Obispo were burned by hostile Indians.

[39]

which we would go our respective ways. Seeing how sensible, legitimate, and easy my proposal was, he took as an excuse not that it was beyond doing but that he had no order from His Excellency and therefore could not supply me anything. Finally, he let me have one of the expedition's horses.

I was persuaded by all this that the Commander had taken it very ill that I had come into these parts, the more since in his response to my letter he had said it did not in the least suit him that the Indians of the Colorado should come through to the establishments at Monterey. A little before my arrival, there had been at San Gabriel for their traffic in shells a few Jamajabs (those I have already said I met). When news of them reached the Commander, he wrote to the corporal at this mission to seize these Indians and take them toward their land a long way from here—an order that was not carried out because it arrived after they had left.

I don't doubt that the Commander must have had solid reasons for his decision, and have formed upon them his judgement that communications and dealings between the nations of the Colorado River and those of the coast would be harmful; but, begging his pardon, I shall say it is so far from being harmful that I rather consider it necessary if we are to carry forward with confidence the project of opening communications between those establishments and these provinces [Sonora and its neighbours].

In every nation, even advanced ones, it is common policy to deny passage to those who are going to favour one's enemies; but since communication between the Colorado River and the coast is a necessity, how are the Spaniards to go through if the nations of the one area are at odds with those of the other? The King our Sovereign orders that all Indians, even those unbaptized, be admitted into the presidios with displays of good-will. How, then, without thwarting His Majesty's intentions, can orders be given to seize them? The law of nations permits trade between one people and another. What reason, then, can there be to stop the harmless and long-established commerce of the river people with those of the sea, consisting as it does in some white shell-beads? If we preach to the heathen a law of peace and charity, how can we think of sowing discord?

[40]

Some of the nations nearest those establishments are justly provoked with the Spanish soldiers because of the abuses they have suffered, especially from deserters. Therefore, if the distant nations become exasperated, and the Indians make common cause, those establishments will not last, nor shall we be able to found others, and thus the wishes of our Catholic King will be set at nought. Because of all this I cannot give assent to the Commander's opinion; rather, it seems to me that it would have been more profitable, as well as correct, if he had ordered that the Indians be treated kindly, so that word of the Spaniards' good conduct should reach their land and spread among the heathen nations.

The Indians I have mentioned were returning contentedly, as I can personally testify, because the priests, the soldiers, and the mission's Indian converts had treated them well. It would have been otherwise if they had told of being seized; besides speaking ill of us to their own nation they would have complained to the Yumas, through whose territory Lieutenant-Colonel Juan Bautista de Anza was to return, and perhaps he would not have had the same good reception as on his outward journey. I have already related that the sudden calm at San Diego was occasioned when the Quemeyás who came with the news found that all the river Indians were now friends with the Spaniards, and at the same time met with the courtesy and kindliness of the Commander of the expedition. This is my view.

With regard to my supplies, the charity of my brothers did what Commander Rivera did not do. They also favoured my companions with presents. So I continued toward my goal, but not by the route past the [Santa Barbara] Channel since the Fathers impressed upon me that it was very risky. I stayed at San Gabriel Mission until April 9.

[SAN GABRIEL MISSION TO THE TULARES]

April 9   *74th day of journey*   *Leagues travelled 1 ½*
I left the mission accompanied by two of its Indians and those I brought with me. After one and a half leagues northwest and west-northwest, I arrived at a ranchería where they received me with high spirits. I preached to them through one of the mission Indians. From here the two of them went back to San Gabriel.

April 10   *75th day*   *5 ½*
I left with a guide from among the heathen Indians and, after going two and a half leagues northwest, came to a ranchería where I ate. In the afternoon I travelled three leagues north-northwest along the foot of the San Gabriel mountain range, which bore to the right.

April 11   This day I stopped here to send for a little book I had left at San Gabriel.

April 12   *76th day*   *2 ½*
I went two and a half leagues to the northwest and with a few excursions I crossed a marsh and two watercourses to arrive at a ranchería. Here, from experience of the passage of soldiers, the young women hid; for although this is not on the usual route, these people go down to the sea and have seen and suffered many abuses. This place is at 34° 13′.

April 13   *77th day*   *3 ½*
I crossed a mountain range running to the west-northwest from the [Sierra] Nevada and after two leagues north I arrived at the Santa

[43]

Clara Valley; then, after one and a half leagues west-northwest, I came to its marsh. Here I stopped until the 23rd because one of the Jamajabs had fallen ill. In the meanwhile I visited several rancherías in these mountains. The ravines and watercourses that I saw had much water and there was abundant pasturage.

I noticed how mild and approachable the people of this nation are. I baptized the old infirm father of the captain of these rancherías, having first with difficulty instructed him through Sebastián. Some Indians from the north-northeast arrived who wanted to take me to their country with five more Jamajabs who had come to trade.

April 23 *78th day*   9
I left toward the west, later turning north and going up over the high mountains, covering altogether nine leagues. I stopped at a marsh on the way down.

April 24 *79th day*   ½
Travelling half a league northeast, I came to a pool and near it a ranchería where there were signs that Captain Pedro Fages had passed that way. The Indians are very mild-mannered, and the women cleaner and neater than the others of this Beñemé nation. In the afternoon two Indians of the north came, of the nation they call the Cuabajai.

April 25 *80th day*   5
Crossing a valley, I came to another high mountain range [the Tehachapi], a branch of the [Sierra] Nevada running northeast, which I called the Sierra de San Marcos, and having gone four leagues to a watercourse, and in the afternoon another league, still northward, I stopped in the same stream-bed. In this mountain range there are lofty pines, oaks, and other trees.

April 26 *81st day*   2½
I went up the Sierra de San Marcos a distance of two and a half leagues north, to where I had sight of lofty mountains and of leafy, grassy canyons. Three and a half leagues more, and I came to some rancherías of the Cuabajai nation where the old women gave me many seeds of chia [the lime-leaved sage], which are abundant here.

This ranchería, which I called San Pasqual, is built thus: There is

[44]

a large square enclosure with arches of willow and a roof of mats made of rushes split and sewn together. It has some windows to let smoke out, but only one door at the east and another at the west, at each of which a guard stands all night. On all sides are sleeping-rooms to which they go when it is time, each family until then staying by the fire at the door of its own chamber.

As I said, it was the old women who welcomed me, because the Jamajabs had gone ahead to give notice of my arrival. The young people, as soon as they heard it was a Spaniard that was coming, took to the woods. When I came up to the ranchería, as one of the Jama-jabs was wearing my woollen shirt and the other my blanket they were suspicious of them, thinking they too were Spaniards; but seeing that they did them no harm and that my companions were not Spaniards but Jamajabs, they all gathered round to have a look, and showed their pleasure by kissing my crucifix and responding to everything I said that it was good.

They told me that in the night the captain had taken all the animals over from the western to the eastern side because there were bad people about. The Jamajabs were grieved that the Indians should question them insistently, above all to ask if I was a Spaniard from the west. They answered no, that they were from the east, and all the nations loved me dearly because I did no harm to anyone; they themselves might have considered me a Jamajab, and that was why they came with me.

At nightfall I went into the large hut, or enclosure, where each family was at its fire. I went from one to another, greeting them cordially, and sat down at the captain's fire. Through an Indian who understood their language well I told the captain that I knew he had a good heart and so would do me no harm, but there were bad people near and he should tell me if there were anything I should know. "Don't be afraid," he answered; "I shall escort you with all my people as far as the next ranchería, and no one will harm you. We already know that you have behaved well toward the people of the great river."

I recited there the Corona and, with Sebastián and the two Jamajabs, chanted the Alabado,[18] as has been my practice at all the rancherías, to their wonderment and pleasure, so that word of it has passed from one nation to another and they would ask me, "When are you going to pray? The people don't want to leave until they have seen you pray and sing." I noticed that no sooner did I begin to pray than all shouting, dancing, and hubbub ceased and they preserved a dead silence. They kept giving me shells in great numbers in exchange for my Corona. This night, as we were praying, the captain's wife took a basket of chia seeds and, as an offering, emptied it over the crucifix at my breast. The other women did the same, and threw some into the fire so there would be a burst of light.

When I had finished reciting the Corona, I sat down with the captain and some old men who gathered near. They sucked on the tobacco I gave them and then asked me to show them my breviary and the compass and other things, with all of which they were delighted. Then the captain took a little white stone out of his pouch and cast it into the fire to be heated, and after it was hot he mashed it thoroughly in a stone mortar, adding water and tobacco until the mixture was like gruel. He handed me the pestle, which was also of stone, for me to lick and taste the broth, which I found most bitter. The moment I gave him back the pestle, he wet it again and handed it to an old man, who took quite a lick but had to force himself to get such bitterness down. Then came my companions' turn. When one of the Jamajabs tried it, he had such a vomiting spell that I thought he would die, which the ranchería people greeted with a burst of laughter. The meeting broke up when there was no other to try it.

I slept near the door of the big hut, and from an Indian on watch I was able to make out that they drink this gruel to banish fatigue and for this reason give it to their guests. Here I saw baskets, flint knives, shallow bowls with inlaid work of mother-of-pearl—the knives had it too—and woven shellwork, all of which things are to found also at the [Santa Barbara] Channel, since there is much trading back and forth and perhaps these Indians belong to the same

18. The Corona is a rosary of seven decades offered to the Virgin; the Alabado, a hymn beginning with that Spanish word, extolling the Blessed Sacrament.

nation; from what I hear, they are similar also in their dress and in the cleanliness of the women.

April 27 *82nd day*   1 ½

I travelled a league and a half west-northwest, accompanied by the captain and all his people; passed through good lands and clumps of trees, along the same watercourse; and came to another large ranchería composed of several big huts like the last. This place is at 35° 9'.[19]

There they received me with great pleasure and fed me generously. They urged me not to go on; even Sebastián and the Jamajabs refused to accompany me. Seeing how reluctant they were, I stayed there until the 30th of April, although in that time I went out twice to have a look at the surrounding country. They were well aware of my desire to go on, but said that the people next them were not related to them and were very bad Noches. However, seeing me unhappy, an old man of that same Noche nation who had taken a wife in this ranchería offered to go with me.

April 30 *83rd day*   8

Telling Sebastián and the Jamajabs to wait for me there the four or five days that I should be away, I set out eastward with the old man. After we had passed some low hills and travelled eight leagues northward, I stopped at a watercourse which I named after Santa Catarina, having met on the way some boys of the Noche nation to whom I gave presents. Right at hand is the Sierra de San Marcos, which runs northeast and north, about eleven leagues distant from the San Luis range. As we were savouring at this place a very tasty herb that grows in the stream-bed, we saw up the mountainside three Noche Indians. The old man went over to speak to them, and seeing that they did not approach I got up to give them presents, but I only succeeded in getting one of them to come a little nearer. He threw me two squirrels; so also did the other two Indians. With these six squirrels, and six others which they gave the old man, we had a supply of food. We went for the night further down the same

---

19. At this point, Elliott Coues's translation goes on as follows: "This was the last observation I made on my journey. I note that for all former observations I availed myself of the tables computed by a religious of my college for the meridian of Sonora."

watercourse, where we found two huts and the families who lived in them.

After a league's travel northwest I came to a big river [the Kern], the waters of which, beautiful and crystal-clear, make a great noise as they issue from the San Marcos range, for where they come from the eastward they are narrowly boxed in. I wanted to cross at once because the river, though rapid, did not seem to me to have much water; but the old man dissuaded me. Continuing downriver, I came to a ranchería where the inhabitants were kind and generous to us, and from there three Indians went with me as far as another ranchería, on the other side of the river, to which they told me I could cross. Difficulties arose when they asked me if I knew how to swim. When I told them no, and that they should make a raft, they answered that they didn't know how. Finally I took my clothes off, except my shirt and drawers; though they urged me to take off even these, I refused. Then they decided to take me across by having four swim me, two holding me by the arms and two by the body; and with that opportunity I had a fine bath in that beautiful water. My mule crossed by swimming; my habit and saddle were taken over in baskets. The people at the ranchería put on a big celebration at my coming and fed me. Happy at their attention and affection, I reciprocated with tobacco and glass beads.

The men make a good appearance. The women are very neat and clean; they take good care of their hair and put it up in a knot over the forehead, and bathe often. They wear skirts of deerhide and wraps of animal pelts; they show little concern, however, about concealing their person.

I dried out my clothes and in the afternoon an Indian captain from the west came to invite me to go there. I kept refusing and they kept urging, so I brought out the magnetic needle, and as they saw that no matter how I kept turning it about, it always pointed to the north, which was the direction I told them I ought to take, they let me go; and they remained looking at one another with wonderment, which is not strange, for when other Indians have seen the compass they have thought it possessed an understanding of its own.

Along this noteworthy river [the Kern], which I called the Río de San Felipe, there is ample pasturage, an abundance of trees, and much irrigable land. Leaving the ranchería and going three leagues partly northwest and partly north, I came to another river [? Poso Creek], not very big, which, to judge by its bed, undoubtedly rises very high when in flood. I called it the Río de Santiago. It has great masses of trees. I spent the night at a ranchería of notably good-looking people. They were very hospitable, and I reciprocated. Since leaving the San Felipe River I have travelled over country so rugged that the old man, tiring, told me at this ranchería that some-one else must go on with me.

In this Noche nation and even in that of the Beñemés the use of the sweat-bath is common. The sweat-house is an underground room covered with sticks and grass, like an oven, with a single window either in its top or side. They go into it and light a fire, and as there is little movement of air the heat and smoke make their eyes water and their sweat pour to the ground. When they can stand it no longer, they come running out and jump into the river, where they take a thorough bath. This is why these people stay clean; but although well formed, they are slender and not hardy enough for travel afoot.

May 2   *85th day*   4½

I went four and half leagues north and stopped at a ranchería where there were some men with beards, among them an old man with a beard so long, thick, and white that he looked like a reverend ancho-rite, the more so when, having asked of me my crucifix, he hung it at his breast. I noticed here that the young girls, and at times even the older women, went about exposed; but neither here nor in any other ranchería did I see any action that was in the slightest degree immodest.

May 3   *86th day*   2½

I went two and a half leagues north accompanied by another Indian, and on the river which I called the Santa Cruz [? the White River] there was a ranchería of about a hundred and fifty souls. They received me with much hubbub, for as soon as they saw me they began to shout "Ba! ba! ba!" slapping their thighs hard. I gave them

[49]

of the little I had with me. As they were kissing the crucifix an Indian came to me and asked in Spanish for cigarette paper. I was much astonished, and he told me he was from the sea, where there were priests like myself. He said he had seen Spaniards in four different places, and that it was four days since he had arrived. When it was his turn to kiss the crucifix, he did so very reverently and then started to preach to the others, making signs to represent a firelock and the act of whipping. It all made me suspect that he was an Indian who had run away from the Monterey missions. At this ranchería a little boy was dying, so I asked his parents' permission and baptized him, which was most consoling. I took him in my arms with tenderness and called him "Little boy"; and then this Indian, pointing toward the west, repeated "*Pare, pare*, little boy," which [because he used the Spanish word *pare*, 'stay'] quite convinced me that he was of the missions.

Noche Indians from the west arrived to take me to their ranchería, but I did not want to go. Others, called Pagninoa Noches, came from the north, but I did not want to go to their land either, fearing that both Sebastián and the Jamajabs might desert me if I did not turn back at once. These Indians told me that in their land they had killed two Spaniards (probably deserters) because they had behaved badly toward their women, and that they had cut off their hands, slit their bodies wide open, cut them in pieces, and thrown the pieces away. They gave me the names of other peoples toward the north, speaking of Choinoc, Copilla, and Buesanet, which I think are rancherías of the same nation. To those northwest of them they gave the names Telam or Torim; and these, they say, kill, have firearms, and have stolen from them some older girls. They also told me that seven days' journey to the north a very large body of water or river [the San Joaquin] runs from the northeast and joins the San Felipe; for when, as I shall relate, the latter divides into two branches, one takes a northern direction. They gave me to understand that the first river was three times as large as the other. They wanted me to go to see it, for all along the way there were good people. I wanted very much to do so as I thought the distance might be only thirty-five or forty leagues since these people judged that it would take seven days, and they travel little because they take many baths and wear no protection on their feet. My final decision was not to go, as much because I had no presents to give as because of what I have already said about Sebastián and the Jamajabs.

Here the Sierra de San Marcos runs northwest and between it and the Sierra de San Luis are to be seen very broad plains which undoubtedly are the Tulares [bottomland reed-marshes] marked by Father Font on his map and mentioned in his diary, since the San Marcos is the mountain range he could see, snow-capped, forty leagues away and to the east of the marshes. Although there is not this distance here, the mountain ranges gradually open in such a way that at last only the Sierra de San Marcos is seen.

[The Tulares to Mojave Crossing]

I went half a league east to a ranchería where they fed me wild rice and urged me repeatedly to stay; indeed, hardly had I arrived when all the girls went to bring grass for my mule, something that no-where else did I see done. I gave them presents from the very little that I had and returned to the ranchería from which I had come. There they refused me a guide, thus obliging me to stay. The little boy I had baptized was dying, so his parents began to weep and some old women to lament; and the weeping and lamenting went on by turns. Other women and children of the ranchería came and made a large circle, in the center of which was a big bonfire. The child's parents began to cry again, and the old women accompanied them in a contralto chorus. They stopped, and the captain with the young men in the circle chanted in a mournful tone but in measured time. They got up without using their hands and, bending over, danced in time to the chant, beating the measure with their feet and letting their arms hang limp. Then they would stretch their arms forward, putting their palms together; then draw them back to the chest; then extend them crossed over each other, palm down; then they would raise their arms and clap their hands; then they would suddenly sit down—following the rhythm of the chant in everything. I went to the little boy many times. His mother had put on him all the shell beads she had, and I placed on his breast a little cross and left them my kerchief for use as a shroud.

The child had not yet died, and because people were still coming to see me they urged me not to go. They still refused to go with me, but as I continued to worry about my companions I resolved to leave alone.

As soon as I left, an Indian caught up with me who guided me to the next ranchería, which was two and a half leagues to the south. Five Indians left here in my company, with whom, travelling two leagues in the same direction and a little southeast through the mountains, I came to the Santiago River. It had more water than when I crossed it before. After travelling three leagues, we halted to eat at a ranchería where they strongly urged me to stop. I did not give in to their entreaties, but went, accompanied by all the men and women, downriver, southwestward to another ranchería. The captain there, a very serious-looking man, urged me to stay. He offered to take me the next day to see a Spaniard who was married to a woman of the Colteche Noches, a short distance to the eastward. He told me that the Spaniard wore on his breast a round object (it might be a medal or a locket enclosing a relic) and that he would name God and tell them that He was in the heavens; that the Spaniard had a small child and was a good-hearted man, and they all loved him, and he lived in harmony with them. The captain gave me to understand that the Spaniard still wore some clothing. I think that probably he is a deserter who, by reason of his mild ways among them, has been allowed to live. This captain gave me some dried bear-meat, and I took leave of him with regret when it was time to go.

Two Indians left with me. Though I wished to follow the flow of the river, they assured me that there was no way through because the canyons were too narrow. I passed a lofty peak; and when the Indians had put me on the path and had pointed out where the ranchería and the river were, they left me although I urged them repeatedly to go on with me. They left me, I judged, not from discontent with me but because they were naked and it was very cold; moreover, they greatly fear the bears that are in large numbers in this land. I gave no thought to these things myself, in my eagerness to reach my companions; but, a short way further on, when night had fallen, I found myself at the brink of chasms where, though I could discern some paths, they were only footpaths on which my mule could not go. At length, God willed that I should get down to a large canyon which I thought would lead to one of the rivers or, at any rate, to the plains on the west. I kept on in the canyon almost all night, winding interminably, and was elated at coming out, when it was day, on the banks of the Santiago River. To this point I had come four and a half leagues west and southwest from the ranchería I had last left.

May 6 *89th day* 3

I went up the river and then turned down again, doubtful of the place where the ranchería was that I was seeking. I saw four Indians, and as soon as they saw me they began to laugh and shout. They sat to rest themselves because they were weighed down by a large amount of meat they were carrying. They tossed me some roasted squirrels and, opening a grey hide that looked like a muleskin, invited me to have some meat. Among the chunks I saw what looked like a mule's head, and it occurred to me that this might be one of my beasts, as Sebastián might have taken a mule to come looking for me. Because they so kindly gave me food, I agreed, upon their inviting me, to visit their ranchería, and went with them three leagues southeast and east, always in the mountains. The ranchería had about a hundred of the same Noche nation, who received me with great pleasure and celebrated my arrival with dancing. Like those to the north, they spoke to me of the married Spaniard and urged me to go see him, saying I would get there in a day and a half; but haunted as I was with visions of some mishap to Sebastián and the mule, all I wanted was relief from my fears.

May 7 *90th day* 3 [? 5]

After travelling three leagues south-southeast, I was at a league's distance above the place where I had crossed the San Felipe River, and a little later I came to the same ranchería. The Indians urged me to go downriver to where I could cross without getting wet. I went southwest therefore two leagues, remarking the great masses of trees, pasturage, and fit places for irrigation, and came to a ranchería

[55]

of about a hundred and fifty souls. At this place the river is divided in two less narrowly channelled branches, and here is a bridge made of two alder trees over which one can cross at some risk. The branch of the river crossed by the bridge flows west-northwest, and further down they say it goes northward until it joins the very big river I mentioned when speaking of the Pagninoa Noches. The other branch is smaller and flows to the west. Both branches, when in flood, spread over vast plains to the northwest and southwest, where they form large lakes and swamps.

This area has beautiful hills, safe from all danger of flooding, that are suitable for building a mission. I called it San Miguel de los Noches. The people, happy at my coming, gave me meat and fish to eat and a sort of caramel cake made from sweetish roots that are plentiful hereabout. While this was going on I was sorry indeed to note that most of the people would not kiss my crucifix because they saw that an old man refused to do so. He said that the tobacco and shell beads were good, but the crucifix was bad and he was afraid of it. An example of that sort readily explains why, when a mission is first begun, the scene may change suddenly from great joy and docility to woes and unavoidable disasters.

They told me that the sea was far away and that they caught their otters in big lakes. They have large deerskins which the Indians from the west come to buy. I met some of the latter, who urged me to come to their land and who did me a good turn by helping to get my mule and my baggage across the river. Although I tried hard with a big stick three varas long to find out the depth of this branch of the river, I did not succeed because the current bent the stick even though it was made fast to the bridge. Sebastián told me afterward that he had sounded the depth by tying a big stone to a hitching-rope seven varas long and paying out the entire length.[20]

May 8   *91st day*   9

I left accompanied by three Cuabajai Indians and others from the mountains who had come there. After we had travelled three leagues

----

20. Coues's translation adds: "The Indians told me Sebastián had been there and that he had gone away with the Jamajabs, and they gave me to understand also that they had killed the mule: all of which added to my concern, confirming my impression when I saw the mulehead and the meat."

south-southwest the mountain Indians left us for their own land and I went on southeast and east with the Cuabajais, through dry lake beds, clumps of trees, and sand hills. The footing was all kangaroo-rat holes, of which there is an infinite number from here northward. My mule stumbled into them several times, and the same mischance befell me also. I lost the compass needle and did not go back to look for it because I dreaded a return over a barren terrain with no path and so plagued with kangaroo rats.

I went six more leagues as far as the territory of the Cuabajais. They were very festive because of my coming; there was a dance that night and the next day. But I was all the time worried at not finding any of my companions here. The next day Luis the Jamajab came with two animals and a message from the captain of San Pasqual asking me to go at once to the captain's ranchería; but as the message also said that Sebastián had gone looking for me along the San Felipe River I decided to await him where I was. In the afternoon he arrived safe and sound.

May 10 I went to the ranchería of San Pasqual, where I found two Jamajabs who had recently arrived (of those who had journeyed with me there remained only Luis and Ventura); they were evidence to me of the regular trade between these nations and those by the sea. The people of the ranchería supplied us with rabbits, ground chia, and some little loaves made with other seeds. Everything was offered with much rejoicing, and I did not half make return with what I gave them. They asked me when I should come back another time. I spoke again with the captain, counselling him not to make war on the Indians of Santa Clara, where he had killed another captain. I tried to persuade them that the Spaniards are good people, but he did not acquiesce in this opinion, giving me to understand that those who passed through stole baskets and other valuables.

An old man came here with others, saying that along the western edge of the mountains women and livestock had been going by and that many other Indians and horses were still coming. I gave a present to this old man.

I tried to persuade the Jamajabs to return with me to San Felipe so that I could go upriver to the Cajuala Chemevets, but they declined, for although it could be done, between there and the country of the Jamajabs were very rugged mountains which their animals could not cross because they were already footsore. However, though this proposal fell through I succeeded in returning by a different route.

May 11   *92nd day*   *2*

I ascended the Sierra de San Marcos by the east and northeast. After going two leagues I stopped at a watering-place which I called the Laguna de San Venancio.

May 12   *93rd day*   *3 ½*

Continuing a league in the same direction, half a league to the northwest, and two leagues southeast, I came to a ranchería where the native speech is different from that of the Noches and Cuabajais. The Jamajabs call these people Cobaji. I suppose they are the same as the Colteche Noches whom I have already mentioned. There were only women and children, who gave us meat and seeds.[21] This land has conifers, oaks, and other trees. The people here are very robust; at least the women whom I saw were so—the men were hunting. They told me that if I should go north-northeast I would find there many of their nation. I stopped here on the 13th.

May 14   *94th day*   *1 ½*

I travelled one and a half leagues southeast and halted in a streambed which I called the Arroyo de la Ascensión. We had to look for the path, as my companions did not know it.

May 17   *95th day*   *6 ½*

Once through the mountain range, I went on six and a half leagues south-southeast over plains that had much grass but few trees and so little water that we did not get enough for ourselves and our animals at the two holes that we found. If these were deepened, however, water could be had in abundance because the plains are marshy.

---

21. Coues's translation adds: "I returned the favour with some small shells, which they prize. The women told me that they fed and looked after us because we were so needy; that their nation was generous, not mean like those of the west. I believe they are right, as the Indians of the west are hard bargainers, even among themselves, they so value and cherish their possessions; but I certainly have no reason to complain about them."

May 18 *96th day* 2½

Travelling two and a half leagues in the same direction over an immense plain that clearly was in former times a lake-bed, I found another hole with a little water in it.

May 19 *97th day* 4½

Four and a half leagues further in the same direction I came to the Río de los Mártires [the Mojave River] near the place where an observation had read 34° 37′.

May 20, 21, 22

I returned the same way as far as the Pozos de San Juan de Dios.

May 23 2

Turning aside and going two leagues east-northeast, I halted at a sandy place where there was a Chemevet ranchería.

May 24 I delayed here because some of the Jamajabs who had come to trade in shells were ill.

May 25 *98th day* 4½

I traveled four and a half leagues east-southeast to pass the region of sands and the Sierra de Santa Coleta [Providence Mountains].

May 26 *99th day* 3

Three leagues east-northeast and I halted at a watering-place with scant supply; I called it the Pozo de San Felipe Neri.

May 27 *100th day* 5

I went on five leagues east and northeast. The mountains have some trees and there is much pasturage.

May 28 *101st day* 3

After one and a half leagues northeast I arrived at a good watering-place which I called the Aguaje de la Trinidad, where there is a Chemevet ranchería. In the afternoon I went on a league and a half southeast and stopped at another ranchería. In the mountains there are large natural basins of water.

May 29 *102nd day* 9

Two leagues to the east I found a waterhole with abundant supply.

Seven more leagues, to the southeast, and I came to the Pozos de San Casimiro.

Travelling two leagues east-southeast, I again entered the country of the Jamajabs. Their joy at seeing me there once more would be hard to describe. They had sent word to the Tejua Yavipais, the Jaguallapais, the Chemevets, and the Jalcheduns, so that upon my arrival and in my presence they could talk together unhurriedly and celebrate peace. Even though they knew I had just received a letter from the Commander [Anza] urging me to return to the Yumas, they wanted me to stay a week. From the running about, the yelling, and the general hubbub of this meeting, and from the great heat, I feared I should fall ill. A general peace was concluded among the nations I have named, to their great pleasure and mine. I spoke at length with the Jaguallapais about the distance to Moqui and New Mexico and they supplied me information about the whole area. I wanted to go there, but the letter I had received obliged me to turn south to the territory of the Yumas.

On the following day [May 31] I took my leave, having given presents to all, especially to the Jaguallapais. As they started for home, some of the Jamajabs who were relatives of the men killed by them in past wars began to shout that they would kill them. The Indians in authority opposed this on account of the newly made peace and on my account too. They brought the Jaguallapais before me, terrified and suspicious (as I was too, for I did not trust the Jamajabs). On the spur of the moment I made up my mind to accompany them, and I told them not to be fearful, for I was going with them. No one opposed my resolve, though it is common enough that serious troubles attend such surprise moves. A Jaguallapai at once went forward with two Jamajabs to advise his nation that I was coming over to that land. Sebastián, who was the sole member of my company, refused to follow me though I begged him hard to do so, and thinking that I might never again see the Jamajab nation I told him to go down with the Jalcheduns to their lands.

[60]

[MOJAVE CROSSING TO ORAIBE PUEBLO]

June 4   *104th day of journey*   *Leagues travelled 2*

I travelled along the banks of the [Colorado] River two leagues northwest and came to the place which I had found on my earlier journey to be at 35° 01'.

June 5   *105th day*   *4½*

After going a league north along the river, I went downstream southward half a league. In the afternoon I set out eastward and went three leagues, mainly to the east-northeast.

June 6   *106th day*   *4½*

I climbed, to the east-northeast, the mountain range that I called the Sierra de Santiago; and travelling one and a half leagues southeast I arrived at the watering-place they call the Aguaje de San Pacífico. There is no lack of pasturage. In the afternoon I continued two leagues south-southeast and another east.

June 7   *107th day*   *4*

I travelled four leagues east and reached the territory of the Jaguallapais, who had a place ready for feasting us. They are of much the same character as the Tejua Yavipais, their enemies. They behaved very well toward me, in keeping with the warmth that I had shown toward them. I gave them to understand that I wanted to go to Moqui. The strongest of objections were raised by the Jamajabs, because they feared that the Hopi Indians might kill me; but my insistence finally prevailed.

At this place there is a little stream-bed with running water, good pasturage, good hunting, and an abundance of chia. I spoke to them of God and saw that they had some knowledge of Him. All of them kissed my crucifix and had their little children kiss it too. They wear garments of deerskin and some blankets from Moqui with Spanish-style sashes. They have awls and other tools given them by the Hopi Indians. I did not see any cultivated fields, and I think they live on mescal and game. I stayed one day.

June 9 *108th day* 6

I went three and a half leagues northeast along the flank of a great mountain range [the Cerbat Range] which I called the Sierra Morena. In the afternoon, going two and a half leagues in the same direction, I stopped at a ranchería. There were with me the captain of the ranchería last visited, with one of his Indians, and a Jamajab whom the captain had assured me no one would harm. In order to get me drinking-water, an Indian woman went to the mountains for it two hours before daybreak. The captain of this ranchería and his wife offered to accompany me.

June 10 *109th day* 6

After five leagues east I came to the Arroyo de San Bernabé, which in some places has running water and in others not. In the afternoon, after another league along this same watercourse in the same direction, I halted at an abandoned ranchería. My companions set fire to a hovel, raising clouds of smoke to see if there were any Indians near. None appeared, so we went on eastward. Soon one of my companions saw at the foot of a tree two children who, when asked where their father was, said he would soon come; and he did, about ten o'clock the next morning, with his wife, greeting us with pleasure. The man, seeing my mule, asked for it, to bring in a buck that he had left dead. It is remarkable how these Indians share whatever they get from hunting; though the amount be small they share it with everyone. On this occasion, before loading the deer on he cut it up and gave half to the captain who accompanied me. The days I stopped there, they both gave me of their portions.

This ranchería belongs to the Yavipais, who differ only in name

VIEW OVER CANYON-FURROWED PLATEAU

Grand Canyon in middle distance; Cataract Canyon coming in from south, at right.

From a drawing by WILLIAM HENRY HOLMES, *1880, reproduced as a chromolithograph in 1882*

from the Jaguallapais. The Indian sent a messenger to his relatives, telling them I was here (four of them had seen me in the land of the Jalcheduns), and therefore he urged me to stay until they should come. On the second day the relatives began to put in an appearance, in troops of six or eight. The chief or head of each troop made a speech upon arrival, to which the Jaguallapai captain who was with me replied. Each captain on ending his speech turned to his men, asking them if what he had said was good, to which they all answered yes. Finally, the Jaguallapai captain said: "This Father has a good heart; he is on close terms with our friends the Jalcheduns; he has made peace for us with the Jamajabs. Now he wants to go to Moqui, and he asks your permission." All acquiesced in my desire, knowing that I was a Spaniard and that the Hopi Indians are on friendly terms with the Spaniards of New Mexico. Then three Indians, two men and a woman, came saying they were from near Moqui and offering to go there with me. They did go part of the way. Their bearing was superior, and their dress so good that they looked quite civilized. From this place my earlier companions turned back.

June 15   *110th day*   4½

Taking leave of the gathering, which was made up of some sixty men (no women or children), I followed the watercourse upstream to the northeast and north and came to a ranchería of about forty souls, where we ate. Then I went on up the watercourse, and at some pools which I called the Pozos de San Basilio [Peach Springs] I came upon some little girls who were there for water with containers that appeared to be made of mulberry wood, common in these parts, which had been coated with gum. I kept on, heading now in one direction, now in another, as far as a ranchería where I spent the night, having travelled that day four and half leagues.

June 16   *111th day*   9

After travelling four leagues northeast and north, with thickets of juniper and pines on either hand, and in the afternoon five leagues to the north, we stopped at a mountainous ridge where the earth was red, and the Indians told me that the Colorado River was near

[63]

by. We saw deep gorges of the same colour. Where we halted there was very little water. The two Indian men and the woman gave me for food some of the mescal they had with them.

This day the married man chanted the Alabado in the same tone as is used at the missions. I was astonished and, giving him a string of beads, asked who had taught it to him. He gave me to understand that the Yutas, his neighbours, knew it because they used to hear it from the Tiguas. He went through it another time or two.

June 17   *112th day*   *2½*

I went two and a half leagues northeast along a very rugged mountain range and arrived at the ranchería where lived the unmarried Indian who accompanied me. He spoke to his captain, who rejoiced at my coming and sent a messenger with news of it to the rancherías toward the north, from which men and women came bringing me gifts of mescal, which abounds in that land. All of them were very festive, danced their fill, and rejoiced over the news that the Castillas (their word for the Spaniards) were tying up the southern Yavipais and taking them far off.

They drew on the ground a sort of map, pointing out all the surrounding nations and the ways to them. They were pleased and astonished when on the same map I outlined my journey. Thus we understood each other, and thus I gained information about all these nations.

The married Indian who came with me, and his wife, set out for their dwelling-place. The way there, they told me, was level and had plenty of water. I could have gone on to Moqui, but they urged me to go to their land, and desirous as I was of seeing more Indians and learning more routes, besides being most grateful for the favours of these companions, I could not refuse.

I spoke to the people of God and of Heaven, and they showed their acquiescence in all that I said. They kissed the holy crucifix and raised it heavenward, and thus it was passed from hand to hand, even to the smallest children. In this and in other rancherías there was not one maimed, sightless, infirm, or exhausted person who failed to entreat me to lay my hands on him and say some prayers for him. I would recite a little of the Gospel, or the Magnificat; and

[64]

so I continued to do throughout the land of the Yavipais. I was not able to discover the origin of this devotion as a means to health. I stopped here one day.

June 19   *113th day*   *3*

I travelled a league east, accompanied by the captain and three others from his ranchería, also one of the important Indians of those along the Jabesua River [Cataract Creek], who had a beard but only a scanty one. I came to a ranchería and near it a waterhole with abundant supply which I called the Pozo de la Rosa because it was overtopped by rosebushes. Throughout this land there are many and large pines. I went upslope northward and after two leagues stopped at a ranchería where the Indians begged me not to go further.

June 20   *114th day*   *10*

I went on five leagues east, two northeast, and three north, the last four over most difficult terrain, through gorges which though immensely deep had abundant herbage and not a few trees, and thus came to a ranchería on the Jabesua River which I called San Antonio. To get to it I went along a narrow way that I called "the new Canfran," some three handbreadths wide with a very high cliff on one side and on the other a hideous abyss. What came next was worse. I had to get down from my mule and the Indians from their horses in order to descend a wooden ladder.[22] All the earth here is red. There are many mescal plants. There are some cows and a few horses, most of them with a brand which I did not recognize; of only one did I have a suspicion that it might be from San Ignacio

---

22. Compare Lieut. J. C. Ives's account of descending this same canyon in April, 1858, in his *Report upon the Colorado River*, pp. 105-109, which includes the following: "Glancing down the side of my mule I found that he was walking within three inches of the brink of a sheer gulf a thousand feet deep; on the other side, nearly touching my knee, was an almost vertical wall rising to an enormous altitude. The sight made my head swim, and I dismounted and got ahead of the mule, a difficult and delicate operation, which I was thankful to have safely performed. A part of the men became so giddy that they were obliged to creep upon their hands and knees . . ." They came to a precipice which the mules could not descend, and had to turn back. A day or so later a further exploration was made and they found below a shelving rock "a crazy-looking ladder, made of rough sticks bound together with thongs of bark." A member of the party started down the ladder, which gave way. However, he discovered at the bottom of the canyon "a narrow belt of bottomland, on which were fields of corn and a few scattered huts"—an Indian dwelling-place that was a direct descendant of the ranchería visited by Garcés.

[65]

Mission. I asked these Indians, as I had asked others, where they got these horses and cows; they answered, from Moqui, where there are stolen livestock and many horses.

I arrived at night. The Jabesua Indians came so decked with pieces of red cloth that I thought they might be of the Apaches who harass these regions, the more since the women came also and among them were some who were whiter than one generally sees in the other nations. I was not afraid, since I saw how joyous they were at my coming and that they were accepting willingly the peace proposed by me with the Spaniards and the Jamajabs. I informed them that the Spaniards would soon come to live on the Colorado River with the Yumas, Jalcheduns, Cocomaricopas, Gileño Pimas, and Noraguas. They urged me so persistently that I had to stop there five days. During this time they treated me to deer-meat and beef, maize, beans, greens, and mescal, with all of which they were well provided.

It pleased me much to see that at daybreak the husband would go out with his wife and older children to work their fields, taking along the tools they needed such as digging-sticks, hatchets, and grub hoes; all these they get from Moqui. They are decently clothed and are fond of remnants of red cloth which they call Spanish because it comes from New Mexico. I think perhaps the women here are so light in color (I saw one who might be taken for a Spaniard) because the place where they live is so deep down that the sun scarcely gilds it before ten o'clock in the forenoon. In all my travels I have seen no better natural stronghold. It contains about thirty-four families and I believe it to be the largest of all the Yavipai rancherías. The Jabesua River flows through here. It rises in the tangled gorges that are in every direction, and runs northwest and north, flowing near here into the Colorado River. It is a medium-sized river but very rapid. The Jabesuas, by means of good dams, draw much water from it to cultivate crops.

June 25   *115th day*   *5*

Accompanied by five Indians I went two leagues south and east with much difficulty, partly on foot, partly on horseback (they had taken our animals out by another path), and halted on the way up

[66]

the heights at a watering-place with scant supply. In the afternoon I got to the top of that most painful ascent (its precipices are horrifying), and after a further three leagues southeast and north over land with much herbage, junipers, pines, and so forth, I arrived at a Jabesua ranchería where they had come to pick juniper berries. The principal man among the Indians said that next day he would go with me.

June 26   116th day   *8*

Four more leagues southeast and south, and I stopped in sight of the succession of very deep gorges among which flows the Colorado River. From here I saw that in a very large mountain range extending from southeast to northwest and blue with distance a deep passage was cut, steep-sided like a man-made trough, through which the Colorado River enters these lands; I called it the Puerto de Bucareli.[23] Although to my sight it seemed quite near, it was very hard to reach on account of the canyons in between. It lay to the east-northeast from where I looked. I saw toward the north some puffs of smoke which I was told were made by the Payuchas, who dwell on the other side of the river.

Here, three families were waiting to go in company with us, since the way is very hazardous because of hostilities with the Tejua Yavipais and the Napacs. These Napacs live in a mountain range of the same name which, starting from that of the Puerto de Bucareli and running west, is in some places very high; it was still covered with snow. I think the Río de la Asunción rises there. This day they showed me some tracks of the Tejua Yavipais which went off to the north since in that direction lies their path for going to trade with their friends the Chemeguavas. After travelling four leagues southeast in the afternoon, we spent the night in a pine forest.

June 27   117th day   *4*

Four leagues to the southeast and east we crossed by way of a depression a large part of the Puerto de Bucareli highland [the Coconino Plateau] and stopped at a waterhole in a secluded place where there is a cave.

---

23. Father Garcés thus named the Grand Canyon of the Colorado in honour of the Viceroy of New Spain, Antonio María de Bucareli y Ursua.

After traveling three and a half leagues southeast, south, and east, I came to the Jaquesila River [the Little Colorado], which I called the Río de San Pedro. It had an abundant flow, but the water was so turbid and red that it could not be drunk. In the pools along its banks there was good water. This river runs west-northwest; its bed, until it joins the Colorado (not far above the Puerto de Bucareli), is a very deep trough in the living rock, about a stone's throw in width, which even an unmounted traveler cannot possibly cross before reaching this place where I was, at which point with much trouble I was able to get down to it. The gorge continues upstream east-northeast, although not so deep. After crossing the river, I travelled eight leagues north in the afternoon through another canyon like the river channel. I had to branch off to reach a ranchería of about thirty Yavipais, who received me most warmly because there was among them the Indian who sang the Alabado as I have related above.

The captain of this ranchería, a noticeably long-bearded man, was the brother of the Jabesua Indian who accompanied me. Two Indians from Moqui had come to trade with these Yavipais. I found them dressed almost like Spaniards; they were wearing leather jackets. One of them kissed my hand. When I gave him a little tobacco and some shells he returned them to me. I called to the other, but he would not come near, nor kiss my crucifix, which the Yavipais offered to him. These Hopi Indians went away early the next morning, but I did not leave until the first of July.

I went one and a half leagues east-southeast and came to a river that seemed to me to be the San Pedro Jaquesila. Near it was a pueblo in ruins. I was told that the pueblo had belonged to the Hopi Indians, and that the signs of crop-raising yet to be seen were their work since notwithstanding the distance from their homes they still come here to cultivate their fields. The river was low, with yellow water. After I crossed the river and some hills, I reached some very wide treeless plains. I travelled over them six leagues in the same direction and came to some of the Hopis' horse corrals, which were gorges or

LOOKING INTO AND ACROSS THE GRAND CANYON OF THE COLORADO
From a drawing by WILLIAM HENRY HOLMES, *1880, reproduced as a chromolithograph in 1882*

ravines not easy to enter or to leave, with not much water. From here the only mountain ranges that can be seen are to the south and southwest; they lead to the Apache country.

July 2   *120th day*   6

I travelled three leagues east-southeast and three more east and south, and came to the pueblo called Muca by the Yavipais, which is Oraibe, the first settlement in Moqui. Meeting a young man, I offered him tobacco but he refused it. Two leagues further on, when I approached, as if to shake hands with them, two Indians who were well mounted and well clad, they drew away making signs to me to go back. The Yavipais with me spoke in my favour, but met with rebuffs and turned to me to ask what I wished to do. I gave the Hopis to understand that if they would not receive me I would go on to the Gualpes or to the Spaniards; and then, without waiting further, I continued forward since the pueblo was near. Of the eight Yavipais who were my companions only an old man and a boy caught up with me, and with them I entered the pueblo. The path up to the mesa is very narrow. Beside it was a sheep corral where they were guarding three flocks. Theirs are bigger than the Sonora sheep, and the black ones have the best colour.

I ascended the slope and went across the mesa, passing some heaps of sand, to a spring that is in front of the pueblo. Although the soil is poor and there is no pasturage on the mesa, I saw many peach trees in the ravines, and at the edge of the spring I saw some beds of onions, beans, and other garden truck which they have cultivated only with much labor.

I came to the pueblo. At the entrance there are two or three tumbledown houses, and in the others neither door nor window is to be seen from this side. I entered through a rather wide street running from east to west as far as the pueblo exit, I think the only one. There come in at the sides of this street others of the same width, which in different blocks open into two small squares. The ground is not even, but it is firm, and the north-to-south streets are level because the slope of the place is toward the east.

The houses are built in storeys, some with more, some with fewer. Their arrangement is as follows. From the street level a wall rises to

[69]

a height of about one and one-half varas, at which level is the court-yard, reached by a movable wooden ladder. The ladder has no more rungs than are needed for climbing to the courtyard, but its side rails reach to the flat roof. On the level of the courtyard there are two, three, or four rooms with wooden doors, bolts, and keys. If they keep chickens, the coop is here. The courtyard wall has a stairway leading to the upper storeys, which have each a big room in the middle and other rooms on both sides. There is also in the same wall a set of steps leading up to the roof, which commonly connects with the neighbouring houses. The noteworthy thing is that all the living-quarters of the houses turn back to, so that no one can see what another is doing indoors unless he climbs up to the roof. The [house] shape is not square, nor is it exactly rounded.

As soon as I had entered and dismounted in the sight of a large number of women and children who were on the roofs, I approached, with the intention of climbing up, a house that was known to the old man; he had been speaking with its mistress, who was on the roof. She told him to come up but to warn me that I was not to come, nor my things either. I went to a secluded place I found by the street and unsaddled. The Yavipai took my mule to a corral for livestock.

All day long there were men, women, and children taking a look at me, but none would come close even though I offered them white seashells, at which their faces would light up because they like them so much. The old Yavipai said to me: "Stay here by yourself. These people don't like you and they are bad." With the corncobs thrown in the street I built a fire and made a little gruel. The rest of the Yavipais arrived and I heard them talking a great deal in the houses, undoubtedly pleading my cause. In the afternoon I saw coming into the pueblo the men returning from work, with their hatchets, digging-sticks, and grub hoes.

At nightfall an old man came to me. I gave him a present and held the crucifix for him to kiss. On receiving the gift he said in Spanish, *"Díos te lo pague* [May God reward you]"; and he went away. Another came, a young man, whom I treated similarly, and he began to say to me in Spanish: "Father, these are savages who do not wish to be baptized, nor do they believe that you are a priest; but I do,

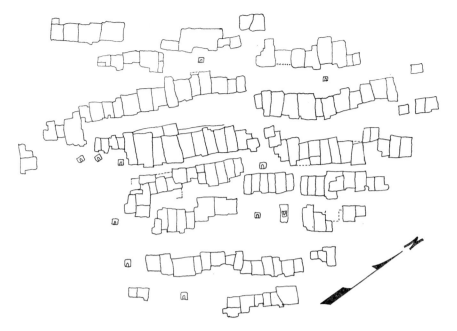

LAYOUT OF STREETS AND BLOCKS OF BUILDINGS IN OLD ORAIBE

TOPOGRAPHIC SITUATION OF ORAIBE PUEBLO
(Other Hopi pueblos on Black Mesa omitted)

because I am baptized, and I am from Zuñi, where all the people are good and are content with their priest. We know that those who are baptized go to Heaven. Our priest came here, too, and when he returned he told us that these people were bad for they did not wish to be baptized. But the priest is satisfied with us of Zuñi. He came a short while ago from Mexico City and the old one went to Santa Fe. There is also a priest in Acoma and Laguna. You can go with us to him tomorrow, for there are three of us. The way is good, with water; it lies toward the sunrise. Before noon we shall arrive at the first pueblo, where there is plenty of fodder and the animals will feed well. Leaving on the next day and with all that day and the night for travel, you will reach the mission; if not, then on the following day. Don't be afraid of the Nabajai Apaches, for they have come down in peace and say that the Spaniards are brave and that a bearded man"—they mean me—"has come saying there is to be war no longer and the mission priest is writing to Santa Fe." I did not answer the Indian on this point; I only told him that I was glad we had met. I asked for the captain of the pueblo, and he said: "The captain doesn't want to come here [to you]. He has hid himself; where, who knows?" I urged him to tell the people that I was a priest, a minister to the Spaniards of Sonora and to other Indians like them. I asked him to say that they should permit at least the children to come near me, that I might give them presents and tell them about God. The Indian got up and spoke in a low voice to those who were near. Afterward, he asked me if I wished to sleep in the house where he was lodged, but I refused the offer since it had not been made by the master of the house.

At night, as the people went up to their roofs, where they sleep, there was much noise of singing and of flutes; but after a while there was silence. Then a high-pitched voice was heard giving a loud and very long oration or sermon. When it ended, the clamour started up again. After another interval a preacher with a harsh voice came out and while he preached there was dead silence. This night the men walked about the streets for two or three hours before dawn, quite as if it were a Spanish town.

After I had lain down, my companions the Yavipais came. I told them I had decided to go to Zuñi, but they said no, that I should return to the Jabesua country; that the Hopis did not want me. Although I offered them white shells with which to buy maize, they did not accept them because the Hopis would not supply it; and furthermore, the two youngest cast back at me the white shells I had given them on the road, from which I concluded that the Hopis had filled them with misgivings about my presents.

July 3   *121st day*   6

At dawn the three Indians from Zuñi came to me. I told them I no longer wished to go to their pueblo because the Yavipais would not go with me and I would not be able to come back through Moqui, doubtful of the Hopis as I was, if I should come without the Yavipais. I had already been advised that the Yutas were friends of the Spaniards, as also of the Yavipais, but the way to them was long, requiring an escort and supplies, neither of which did I have. Besides, it held many other uncertainties if these things should be refused me in New Mexico, as might happen if the Governor should hold the same opinion as Commander Rivera and consider my coming there as harmful and of no benefit to the King's service, especially since His Excellency [the Viceroy] had not expressly commanded it. In the end, I wrote to the Father Minister at Zuñi although I did not know his name, telling him of my coming to this pueblo and of how badly, in contrast to other nations, these Indians had received me. I begged him to send my letter or a copy of it to the Governor and to the Rev. Father Custodian, to whom I sent warm regards. They left me to give this letter to the men at Zuñi.

A little later my old Yavipai Indian came with one of the important men of the pueblo to urge me to go see the other pueblos of Moqui where they would give me something to eat, since here they would not do so. I saddled my mule and, accompanied by the two Yavipais and by many boys and girls as onlookers, went down the slope from the pueblo on the east side, where they pointed out the way to the other pueblos. I demurred, for want of a guide, but the old Yavipai said to me that both I and my mule were hungry and that he would wait here for me five days, as he had not finished selling the mescal and other things he had brought.

I resigned myself to going on alone and entered a vast sandy plain to the south. On both sides of my path I saw many fields of maize and beans, and many Indians working them. I went up another mesa and came upon two little shepherds guarding sheep and a woman with her hatchet getting kindling-wood. They ran off at my approach, which made me sensible of the antipathy of all these people. Reflecting that "Better the known evil of the present than the uncertain good of the future," and, in fine, that my friends the Yavipais were in Oraibe, I decided to go back there. After retracing the three leagues I had covered, I entered Oraibe at nightfall, astonished that so many were on the roofs watching me as I passed by on my mule seeking the secluded place where I had spent the preceding night, which I found after several turns.

In this pueblo the people are of two kinds and two languages: the first can be distinguished by the colour and stature of both men and women; the second, by the difference in the mode of singing. Some are lighter and clearer in colour, and well set up; others are small, dark, and ugly. When they go out from the pueblo they look like Spaniards in their dress, with leather jackets, tight sleeves, trousers, and boots or shoes. Their weapons are arrows and spears. In the pueblo they go about in shoes, and in sleeves of a spotted cloth and a dark-grey blanket such as they themselves make. The women wear a long, sleeveless smock and a grey or white blanket like a square mantilla. The smock is tied round the waist with a sash that is commonly of many colours. They neither daub nor paint themselves, nor did I see beads or earrings. The old women wear their hair in two braids and the younger ones in a whorl over each ear or all tied at one side. They take very good care of their hair.

Although they showed me no favour, I got the impression that among the Hopis there were many good people and that only their rulers were prejudiced. There may have been other reasons for the way I was received, apart from their not wishing to be baptized or to have Spaniards in their lands; for example, hearing that I came from the Jamajabs and the Yumas, friends of their enemies, they may have thought me a spy of the Tejua Yavipais and Chemeguavas. They may also have heard that I came from the land of the Pimas and was minister to them, with whom they are at war, as the Indians of my mission had told me; from which, and having in mind the ruins that are found on the Gila River, I conjecture that Hopi territory once extended to there. Years ago, I asked some old Subaipuris of my mission: Who had built the houses now in ruins and made the earthenware that was now in fragments at the Gila River, since neither the Pimas nor the Apaches know how to do so? They answered: The Hopis, for only they knew how to make those things. They added that these Apaches near by are not relatives [of the Hopis]; that there are many more [Hopis] further north where formerly they [the Subaipuris] used to go to fight though not climbing the mesas where those [Hopis] lived.

This information is confirmed by the fact that when I was among the Yavipais they brought me a large earthenware cup to drink from that bore a likeness to the potsherds in the House of Moctezuma [the Casa Grande]. When I asked where they had obtained it, they answered that in Moqui there are many of them. As I did not go into any house [in Oraibe] I was not able to see them, but from below I did see on the roofs some big painted earthen jars. Moreover, the Gileño Pimas have told me that formerly the Apaches of the north would come to fight them at the reputed House of Moctezuma. As it is certain that the Indians we know as Apaches have no house or fixed dwelling-place, I am persuaded that it was probably the Hopis who came to fight; and that they, harassed by the Pimas, who have always been many and brave, abandoned these communities on the Gila River as they had deserted the pueblo that I saw in ruins before reaching Moqui. They retreated to where they now live, at a favourable site well defended and safeguarded against any invasion.

Within the pueblo I saw no water, but on the eastern slope I saw a copious spring with steps of worked stone leading to it and a curbing of the same material. In my secluded corner I slept that night. One of the Yavipais took my mule to the same corral as on the previous day.

July 4   *122nd day*   *12*
As soon as day began to break I heard singing and dancing along the streets. The dance passed the place where I was and I saw some Indians with feather ornaments on their heads, and other finery, making a din with small sticks on a shallow wooden basin, in com-

pany with flutes. Many followed them and stopped here and there to dance. When the sun was up a great throng moved toward me and made me fear for my life. In the lead came four of the principal men, the tallest of whom demanded of me, with a smile: "Why have you come here? Don't stay. Go back to your own land." I made signs to them to be seated, but they did not wish to do so. I stood up, crucifix in hand, and partly in Yuma, partly in Yavipai, partly in Spanish, and with signs, which are the best language, I made known to them the path of my journey, the nations I had seen, and those that had passed the crucifix from hand to hand and had been good to me. I said, moreover, that I cherished the Hopis, and that I came to tell them that God is in Heaven and that the Crucified was God, Jesus Christ, who was good. To this an old man, contorting his features, said in Spanish, "No, no." At that I said, "Fetch my mule." When it was brought and my things were loaded on I mounted and, with a smile on my face, praising their pueblo and their dress, I left, surrounded by all the crowd until I was beyond the houses.

[Oraibe Pueblo back to Yuma Crossing]

[*July 4, cont.*] I started back by the way I had come, and then I got lost by taking the way to the Yutas, who live to the north and are enemies of this pueblo of Oraibe and of the Muqui Concabe, but not of the other Hopi Indians. The names of the Moqui pueblos are (in the Yavipai language) Sesepaulaba, Masagnebé, Jano, Gualpa, Muqui Concabe, and Muca, as it is called by the Zuñis, which is Oraibe, the pueblo where I was.

I learned that I was going the wrong way from two Hopis whom I came upon; they good-naturedly put me on the right course. When I offered them tobacco and shells they would not accept them; and it was the same with a shepherd, and with two others who were coming from the corrals with horses. In these corrals I got lost again and could not discover a way out until the Yavipais found me; they had stayed in the pueblo, and came out soon after I took my leave. Before they got to me they began shouting "Jatapaiña," which means Pima, and laughing aloud; and went on "How is it that you, Pima that you are, have come into this country?" from which I gathered that the worst obstacle where the Hopis were concerned was to come from the Pimas. Then they began to urge me to move faster, pointing to dense puffs of smoke that could be seen above the land of the Tejua Yavipais or Apaches, who were assembling for war. After nightfall, having travelled twelve leagues west-northwest, we

[77]

came to the Río de San Pedro de Jaquesila, where for supper the Yavipais gave me some tortillas they had brought from Moqui, not much thicker than sacramental wafers and resembling our tortillas of larger size.

July 5   *123rd day*   *1 ½*

I reached the Yavipai ranchería after going one and a half leagues west-northwest. The bearded captain and his people were very sorry that the Hopis had given me nothing to eat, and they did even better for me than on my setting out. They had killed a buffalo [!] and one of the stray cattle; they gave me a share. (Now I realized that it was a buffalo's head that I had thought was a mule's—as I say for May 6.)

They told me that they did want peace with the Jamajabs and that they were paying attention to me and believed what I told them. They also told me of some they call Guamuas, who were friends of the Hopis and enemies to them. They mentioned others, moreover, whom they called Guañavepe; others they called Gualliva; others, Aguachacha (these are enemies of the Yavipais). I asked if the Lipan Yavipais were good and they said yes. I also asked if the Natajé Yavipais were good and they said yes. From this I gathered that their horses came from the Lipan Yavipais or from other Yavipais with whom they are at odds, and that their only enmity is with the Tejua Yavipais, who live in the mountain ranges of the Río de la Asunción. For the vicinity of the Colorado River they mentioned, besides the Yutas and Chemeguavas, some they call Payuchas, and others, Japul, Gualta, and Baquioba. I suppose these are but rancherías of the one nation, as the people are all Yavipais.

They wanted to detain me here forcibly for six days, telling me I was hungry because I had not eaten at Moqui; that they had plenty of meat, and that they were pleased with me. However, I did not accept their favours.

July 6   *124th day*   *4*

I travelled southwest four leagues and came again to the Río de San Pedro Jaquesila.

July 7   *125th day*   *2*

I went on two leagues northwest and west and stopped near the cave where I halted when going in the other direction and the Indians had much buffalo and deer meat.

July 8   *126th day*   *4*

I climbed the mountain range and passed the flat and headed toward the Jamajabs' country by the shortest and easiest way. I told the Indians that I first wanted to go to their dwelling-place because they had been so good to me. This day I travelled four leagues west and southwest and we stopped at a watering-place with abundant supply which I called the Pozo de Santa Isabel.

July 9   *127th day*   *8*

Five leagues northwest, and three more from making turns west-northwest, and I arrived after nightfall at a ranchería in the canyons of the Jabesua River. The descent is very toilsome, but afterward the way between the cliffs is even. They were very happy to see me and urged me so to stop with them that it was six days before I could leave. All this time they looked after me and fed me very well. They took great pleasure in hearing me chant the Litany, and they even learned some of it. To interest them more, when I mentioned St. Anthony I would say "Sancte Antoni de Jabesua"; and St. Peter, "Sancte Petre Yavipai." They made much of this, asking me repeatedly "And I, how?" So I had to assign to each one a saint, from which all learned their names and chanted what they learned.

July 15   *128th day*   *5*

I set out westward. Although the Indians tried to persuade me to go back by way of the ladder, nevertheless, in order to learn if there was an easier way out I was insistent about taking the trail by which they had brought out the horses, which has to the south of it a rugged and bare mountain range. In the end, I came out by the "new Canfran," having travelled south five leagues.

July 16   *129th day*   *6*

I went six leagues west, as far as the Pozo de las Rosas.

July 17   *130th day*   *6*

Leaving toward the southwest and passing the Sierra de los Pinales de San Diego, I arrived in the afternoon at the Arroyo de San Alejo, where I spent the night at a ranchería of Cuercomache Yavipais. They received me well on account of the information they had from others and from the Jabesua Indians travelling with me. This day I met four Yavipais who by order of their captain had come looking for me, fearing that I had been delayed by some difficulty, which shows the great affection the Yavipais had for me. On this day I left the trail that I had been following on my way out.

July 18   *131st day*   *5*
I travelled downstream a league and a half northwest and then, having crossed over some low hills, came out at a little valley which I called the Valle del Lino because wild flax grew there in profusion. (Since I had left Aragón I had not seen this useful plant.) After three and a half leagues west I arrived at a ranchería where I feasted on pine nuts, abundant thereabouts. The Indians made me stay a day so that others might see me.

July 20   *132nd day*   *6*
I went half a league north as far as the watering-place of the ranchería that I called Santa Margarita and, having passed on the west the mountain range that I called the Sierra Morena, two leagues further on I came to a waterhole that I named the Pozo de las Avispas because there were many wasps there, and entered a valley four leagues wide. Four leagues more and I arrived at the ranchería whose captain was accompanying me. I stopped there three days.

July 23   *133rd day*   *2*
Going along the slope of the range two leagues to the southwest, I came to a waterhole and ranchería.

July 24   *134th day*   *7*
I climbed the east side of the range, going two leagues, and then, after a league north, I came to a ranchería where we were fed. Here are two waterholes, and a valley can be seen in the vicinity of the river. From the country of the Jamajabs upstream, the river flows through formidable canyons. In the afternoon I covered four leagues, arriving at a settlement of the Cuercomaches that has a watering-place.

[80]

July 25   *135th day*   *5½*

I travelled two leagues southwest, reached the Sierra de Santiago, which I passed on the west, and went on as far as the waterhole that I called the Aguaje de Santa Anna; later, after a league and a half southwest, I came to the Colorado River, and following its current southward two more leagues I reached the edge of the Jamajabs' territory. As soon as they saw me, these people ran to embrace me, jumping with joy and telling me they had mourned me as dead because it had been reported to them that the Hopis had killed me. Moreover, they had advised the Cuercomaches that if I should return they [the Cuercomaches] should come with me. The Jamajabs also told me that Sebastián was bad, that he had given away the shells and other things I had left; that one of the mules had drowned and another had died. They never stopped talking and touching me.

I was accompanied this far by the captain of the Cuercomaches, a warrior who had served me as an interpreter with the Yavipais and knew the Jamajab language, and two Jabesua Yavipais who were bringing blankets, sashes, and strips of hide to exchange for white seashells. They all stayed on at this place. I gave to each a most hearty farewell, especially the Jabesuas, to whom I owed so many favours. I wanted to give presents to all my travelling companions, as the good company they had given me merited, but I had nothing, so I commended them to the Jamajabs of this ranchería, urging them to be true friends all their lives and to keep the peace that had been established. I have worked much for peace, as my account shows. It can forestall many deaths and the destruction of these nations to whom I owe affection, as well as facilitate the founding of missions and the securing of the desired passage between Monterey and New Mexico. The benefits if the nations are at peace, and the harm if they are at war, are plain to see.

July 26   *136th day*   *2½*

I travelled two and a half leagues southward, downriver, and came to a ranchería that I named San Pedro.

July 27   *137th day*   *1*

After continuing a league south I came to another ranchería, for all this country is populated.

[81]

After three leagues southeast I came to the Ranchería de la Pasión, where I stopped two days because everyone wished to see me. Here I was told that the Tejua Yavipais were now friends of the Coco-maricopas, through whose land I could depart in four or five days' time without going to that of the Yumas. However, as I knew that the Yumas had killed three Jalcheduns, which had provoked much anger, I preferred to take the trouble of making a circuit and visit-ing them all, in order to reconcile them, and at the same time to learn the disposition of the Jalcheduns toward receiving religious instruc-tion and becoming subjects of His Majesty, which is my principal commission with respect to the nations of the Colorado River. Here I baptized three infirm old men and a little girl who was dying, and with new and convincing statements I again affirmed to the Jama-jabs the truth of all that had been said.

Travelling two leagues south-southwest, I came to other rancherías. This day a Tejua Yavipai came as representing his people to learn of my arrival and invite me to their land, where they had been expecting me for days and therefore had stored the carcasses of many ownerless stray sheep. He had no sooner given his message to the Jamajabs than he left without my seeing him as I had wished to do in order to give him gifts and to send a message to his nation explaining why for the present I could not go there.

I went two leagues south as far as the Sierra de San Ildefonso [the Mojave range], which crosses the river, in order to reach the lands of my dear and especial benefactors the Jamajabs. Theirs is the nation that seems to me the nearest ready, and in situation best adapted, for two missions.

I travelled downriver fourteen leagues south, over a rugged land with few trees and no pasturage. On the last day [August 5] I came to a river [the Bill Williams] that I named the Río de Santa María. Its bed is very wide, but at this time it was only half full of water.

Along its banks are pasturage and every sort of riverland tree; so far as the eye could make out, it came from the east at the foot of a great mountain range.

Aug. 6, *142nd day* 14
7, 8

After travelling fourteen leagues south I reached the first Jalchedun rancherías, to which on my earlier journey I had given the name of San Antonio. The Indians behaved most handsomely toward me, and in the King's name I appointed one of their head men a magistrate (I did the same with the Jamajabs) because I found them willing to receive priests and Spaniards. The old men said to me: "We don't have less affection for the Spaniards than the Yumas have. You could well have come through here, since we also have a way to the Jequiches"—they are the Danzarines—"as well as to the Jenigueches" (who are of the Valley of San José and Santa Anna).

I assume that these Indians wear clothes because, besides growing some cotton, they bring in, from Moqui, blankets, sashes, and a coarse woollen cloth, and so have clothing for themselves and for trade with the Jamajabs, Yumas, and Jenigueches.

This day the two girls whom I ransomed and, as I related some days ago, sent back with my old interpreter, came to see me very joyfully. The older one brought firewood and cooked what was given me, which pleased me greatly. I stayed here the 9th and 10th.

Aug. 11 *143rd day* 2

I went on two leagues west-southwest as far as the rancherías of Santa Coleta, near the river, very rich in crops. The heat was excessive.

Aug. 12 *144th day* 2½

I went on two and a half leagues south-southeast and slept at the ranchería near the Laguna de la Trinidad which I mentioned on my other journey to this place. I stayed a day to talk with the old men, my friends of long standing. A Cocomaricopa came, saying that the Tejua Yavipais had killed five Cocomaricopas. I was very sorry to hear this news and took occasion from it to denounce the Cocomaricopas' ugly custom of giving concubines to the Yavipais, as I was aware that they did. And I warned the Jalcheduns that, should a

Tejua Yavipai come to their land, they should not permit him to reconnoitre their rancherías even though he should come with peaceful intent; that they should give him something to eat and then send him back. I told the Jamajabs who were there that they should advise the Tejua Yavipais not to harm the Cocomaricopas, for should they do so they would be enemies of the Spaniards. I marvel at the straight face with which the Cocomaricopa told this lie about the killings, for later I learned that it had been just the opposite.

Aug. 14   *145th day*   ½
I crossed the Colorado River on a raft and went half a league southwest, arriving at an inhabited place which I named the Ranchería de la Asunción. This night I was robbed of five things. The next day I sent a message across the river to the old men asking them what the robbery meant; what would the other nations say, etc. This roused them and they recovered the stolen things. My cloak came back in rags; but everything was accounted for. I stopped here the 15th.

Aug. 16   *146th day*   1 ½
I travelled one and a half leagues south, with some turns to the southwest, and stopped at a ranchería.

Aug. 17   *147th day*   1
I travelled one league southwest and south and halted at a ranchería where one of the principal captains lived. Like all the rest, he treated me well. As by this time ripe ears of maize were plentiful, they feasted me accordingly. To this ranchería and the surrounding ones I gave the name Las Lágrimas de San Pedro [St. Peter's Tears].

Aug. 18   *148th day*   1 ½
I went on one and a half leagues southwest and halted at a ranchería where I stayed one day.

Aug. 21   *149th day*   2
I continued two leagues south-southwest and one southwest. There is a ranchería.

Aug. 22   *150th day*   *1*
I made the river-crossing by raft and went on one league south.
There are small groups of huts.

Aug. 23   *151st day*   *1½*
After going one and a half leagues south, I slept at the last of the
Jalchedun rancherías. Here I met some Yumas who had come just
to wander about in spite of the three Jalcheduns killed in their territory because they had stolen some Yuma horses; but everything was
now fixed. The Jalcheduns assured me that if it were not for the
peace they would have gone down to avenge their relatives; but that
they no longer wanted war; even though the friends of the dead men
asked for vengeance, the rest would not give consent. With it all, so
limited is their understanding that I cannot vouch for their main-
taining the peace.

Aug. 24   *152nd day*   *4*
I travelled four leagues south-southeast although the river runs
southwest. I stopped one day visiting families of the Yumas and
Cajua Jalcheduns.

Aug. 26   *153rd day*   *8½*
I crossed the river, and after half a league south and one league west
I halted at a large natural basin in the mountains. In the afternoon I
travelled two leagues west and at night five leagues south over rough
terrain.

Aug. 27   *154th day*
After going four leagues southeast I arrived at the Puerto de la Concepción, where the Yuma nation received me with special rejoicing
because they too had wept for me as dead. They urged me not to
leave their land, because, they said, in the next month the Spaniards
were coming there to live. They were very sad because under a
mask of peace the Cocomaricopas had killed deceitfully seven Tejua
Yavipais, their friends. That was how I had knowledge of the Cocomaricopa Indian's lie. I denounced this treachery and I charged
Pablo, who was governing in Palma's absence, to tell the Tejua Yavipais, his friends, that I was sad about the deaths of their relatives.
Because I had no gifts I was not going to them, but I was always

their friend and later I would visit them. I told Pablo to maintain the peace[24] with all his neighbours.

The river called by the Yumas the Javill and by us the Colorado is markedly peculiar in the slow rate of its rising and falling in the course of a year. It begins to rise toward the end of February and continues to do so in March, April, May, and June; then it falls in the remaining months, until the following February. Its source is far to the north and even at its beginnings it has quite abundant waters; from the land of the Yutas to its mouth no rivers of importance flow into it except the Gila and the Asunción. I have already mentioned the smaller rivers that run into it further up. The information I have acquired about it is simply this. I asked if in its northern and northwestern parts it was joined by any big river and all the Indians told me no. In what I have seen of it there is no place where it can be forded on horseback except, when it is low, in the land of the Yumas; and here the fording is dangerous and irregular: last year there could not be found the ford where we had crossed the river the year before. Everywhere it has groves of willows, cottonwoods, mesquites, and screw mesquites, except where it passes between rock walls. Although it is wanting in pasturage it does have some short grass and an abundance of reed grass, swamps of rushes, wild amaranth, and other tall fodder grasses. The land along its banks is good except here and there an alkaline stretch. All sorts of crops are to be found, and in places the cultivable lands are so extensive that they can support the inhabitants and many others besides.

The river forms a great rampart for the Yavipais and the mountain Indians because no one dares to cross unless he is taken over by the people of the region. This shows what little fear need be had of the Apaches if our establishments are set up on the further side. The known nations who inhabit its banks are, in order from its mouth: Cucapá, Jalliquamai, Cajuenche, Yuma, Jalchedun, Jamajab, Chemeguava, Yavipai, Payuchas, and Yutas.

What I have said of crops applies only as far as the country of the Jamajabs, since from there upstream the narrow confines of the river do not permit cultivation. The nations along its banks are of good

24. At this point, "666 leguas" is written in the margin as the total of leagues travelled. The addition is not correct; but the right one proves elusive.

physique; even the women are stout and healthy. They are the most numerous and also the richest, wherefore all others desire their friendship. The men, as far as the country of the Jamajabs, go completely naked; the women wear only skirts made of bark. After passing the Jamajabs one finds all the Indians, both men and women, quite decently clad. They bathe in all weathers and do up their hair in various shapes. They are of a generous turn and are fond of their land, so abundant in its products that they forego the hunt. This last comment applies only to the places where the land is cultivated.

When I arrived, the Yumas told me that a Spaniard had drowned because he would not wait for the Indians to take him across.[25]

[Yuma Crossing to San Xavier del Bac]

[*Aug. 27, cont.*] I left these rancherías to return to my mission by the way I had come with the expedition. I first visited the rancherías of the Opas, before whom I condemned the breach of faith with the Tejua Yavipais; but at the same time I intimated that it was not advisable to make peace until the Spaniards should come to their land and the good faith of the Tejuas be tested. They might well fear them if they permitted them to come in and look over their rancherías.

I arrived among the Gileño Pimas accompanied by the Cocomaricopa governor. There was much rejoicing, because the rumour of my death had come even to here. The Pima governor told me that all the [outlying] relatives were very happy and wished to join with the rancherías and have a feast. I agreed, on condition that they do so at a distance from me—guessing what was going to happen. Soon I heard them singing in one confused chorus; then silence, and a few voices were heard saying: "We are good, we are happy, we know God, and we are people who can fight the Apaches. We are glad that the old man"—that is what they call me—"has come back and that the Apaches have not killed him."

---

25. Coues's translation adds: "Among the Quabajais, near the Tulares, I had myself known to have passed a Spaniard on foot, who struck out for the sierra; he who could proceed to the Cajuenches and be the drowned one. The Yumas wished to take me to Caborca, but I desired rather to return by the same route I took with the expedition." There follows a somewhat different statement of what continues in the present translation as far as our next paragraph.

As the yelling grew loud (something foreign to the gravity of the Pimas) I knew at once that it was caused by drink, which produced various effects: some would come and greet me, taking my hand; another would say, "I am Pedro's father"; another, "You must baptize my little one"; another would half pronounce, "Your dwelling-place is here; don't go to see the King, nor to Tucson"; others would half bless themselves in Spanish. Although I was disgusted at the general drunkenness, I was pleased at these expressions which broke from them even in their condition. I was yet more pleased to see that not one woman got fuddled; on the contrary, some of them were picking up, lest they be lost, the clothes and beads that their husbands were throwing away; this they did as they went along guiding by the halter the horses the men were riding. The next day I reproached the governor for the excessive drunkenness. He answered me: "This very seldom happens and only at the time of harvesting the giant cactus, which makes my people vomit yellow and puts them in good bodily condition."

I finally arrived, on September 17, 1776, at my Mission of San Xavier del Bac, where I gave thanks to God and to my patron saints for having preserved me from every ill.

REFLECTIONS ON THE FOREGOING

ALTHOUGH I have said something in the Record about the nations I have seen, and about others from hearsay, nevertheless, since they are many and scattered I have not been able to make proper report of them; nor would that have been possible in a day-to-day record, for it has happened that I have come to understand in the nation next visited what I had not understood when in the one I had just left. Moreover, subsequent happenings have made me now and then doubt the truth of something earlier vouched for. And when I have been twice in some parts, I have still found noteworthy things.

I have not had an interpreter for every nation, but I have confidence enough in the information gathered: on the one hand because I understand sufficiently well the common sign language, and on the other because of the special expedient, which the Indians gave me, of drawing a map on the ground so that it became clear what routes I had travelled and what nations I had seen. Thus we came to mutual understanding. With wonderment at my quick comprehension they distinguished with the clearest of signs even which nations were enemies and which were friends. I availed myself of these same means to learn what nations lay ahead in all directions. In dealing with directions the Indians are very intelligent, and from experience I know that they never make a mistake and that one can be guided in detail by what they say. For these and other reasons I have decided to prepare the following Reflections, bringing together all the information I have acquired and touching upon other points that seem to me useful.

FIRST POINT

Nations Which I Have Visited and of Which I Have Gained Information, and Numbers of Souls Therein

Gila River			Colorado River		
NATION	SOULS		NATION	SOULS	
Pápago	4,000	} A	Cucapá	3,000	} C
Pima	2,500		Jalliquamai	2,000	
Cocomaricopa	2,500	B	Cajuenche	3,000	
			Yuma	3,000	} B
			Jalchedun	2,500	
			Jamajab	3,000	B*

Total of souls, 25,500

[89]

Nations Which I Saw and of Which I Had Information, from the
Jamajabs Upstream on Both Sides of the Colorado River

Northwest and North		*South and Southeast*	
Cajuala Chemegue		Jaguallapai	
Sevinta [MS: Sevicta] Chemegue	D	Cajuala Yavipai	
Chemeguava		Cuercomache Yavipai	E
Chemegue		Javesua Yavipai	
Payuchas	E	Muca, or Oraibe, Yavipai FG	
Yutas			

NOTE: When nations share the same letter it means that they have one and the same language, and if the letter has an asterisk it means that their language differs only in some words.

I was given information that north of the nations I have mentioned there are found the following:

Guamoa	Aguachacha	Baquioba
Guañavepe	Japul	Gualta
Gualliva		

Nations of the mountains of California between the Colorado River and Monterey, near which they have their settlement or the territory in which they wander:

Cuñeil	this nation borders on San Diego and on the mouth [of the Colorado River]	H
Quemeyá	this, on San Diego and on the three first nations of the [Colorado's] mouth	Y
Jecuiche	this, on the Puerto de San Carlos and land of the Jalcheduns	
Jenigueche	this, on the land of the Jalcheduns and Santa Anna	J
Beñemé	this, on San Gabriel and Santa Clara, and on the lands of the Chemeguavas and Jamajabs	
Cuabajai	this, on the [Santa Barbara] Channel and, at the east, on the land of the Cobajis	J*
Noche	this, on San Luis [Obispo] and on the land of the Cobajis	K
Cobaji	this, at the west, on the land of the Noches; at the east, on the land of the Chemegues	L

The area between the Colorado and Gila rivers is occupied by the Tejua Yavipais and other Yavipais. To the south of Moqui all the Indians are Yavipais who are the same as Apaches; from which one realizes how large a territory this nation occupies. The number of souls assigned is scant because I was never able to see the entire nation. Of others I have not estimated the number, either because I was only in the first of their rancherías or because I met them in the lands of other nations; but from the information supplied I infer that none are so numerous as those of the Gila and the Colorado.

In the names of the nations there can be, and usually is, much variation;[26] for example, the Cocomaricopas and Jalcheduns call the Jamajabs "Cuesninas" or "Cuisnurs," while all the rest call them Jamajabs. The Gileño Pimas call the Yavipais "Taros" or "Nifores." The Jamajabs call them Yavipais, and we call them Apaches.

I will say also that the dominant and most warlike nations are, in order: on the Gila, the Pimas; on the Colorado, the Yumas, Jalcheduns, and Jamajabs.

In no nation have I found any signs of [organized] religion; I have seen some medicine men, and they have their superstitions, but I surmise that they have no formal idolatry.

SECOND POINT
Friendly and Hostile Nations

At present all the nations of the Gila and Colorado rivers are at peace, as also are those around them except the Tejua Yavipais, enemies of the Pimas and Cocomaricopas. I cannot say certainly that the peace will continue and hence I shall set down all the old friendships and enmities that may again prevail.

First: the Cucapás have always been friends of the Cuñain [? Cuñeils] and enemies of the Pápagos, Jalliquamais, and Cajuenches.

The Jalliquamais are friends of the Cajuenches, Quemeyás, and Jalcheduns, and enemies of the Yumas and Pápagos.

The Yumas are always friends of the Jamajabs, Tejua Yavipais, and Pápagos of Sonoitac, and enemies of the Jalcheduns, Cocomaricopas, Gileño Pimas, the Indians at the [Colorado] river mouth, and the Jequiches of the mountains.

The Jalcheduns are always friends of the Cocomaricopas, Gileño Pimas, northern Pápagos, Yavipais as far as Oraibe inclusive (except the Tejuas), Jequiches, and Jenigueches, and all the nations from the Yumas southward, and they have been enemies of the Jamajabs, Tejua Yavipais, Chemeguets, and Yumas.

---

26. Variations in Indian nomenclature are notorious. Father Garcés is quite consistent in the names he uses, and seldom departs from the spellings he has once adopted. Most of his important Indian names are not beyond the modern reader's recognition; exceptions are "Yavipais" for Yumans of upland Arizona ("Tejua Yavipais" he equates with Apaches), "Jamajabs" for Mojaves, "Jalcheduns" for Halchidhomas. For further guidance one may wish to consult the appropriate works of Spier, Kroeber, and other ethnologists who have wrestled with this problem.

The Jamajabs have been friends of the Yumas, Tejua Yavipais, and, on the other side of the river, the Chemeguets, and all the nations as far as San Gabriel and San Luis [Obispo]; their enemies have been the Yavipais except the Tejua, the Jalcheduns, Jenigueches, and Jequiches.

The Hopis of Oraibe are friendly with all the Yavipais between the Gila and the Colorado, except the Tejua; with the Yutas; and with the rest of the Hopi pueblos, the missions of New Mexico, and all the southern Yavipais, who are the Indians that overrun these provinces; their enemies are the Tejua Yavipais, the Yutas of the Colorado, the Chemeguavas, the Yumas, the Jamajabs, the Gileño Pimas, and the Cocomaricopas.

The Yavipais of the way to Moqui are friends of [the Hopis of] Oraibe, and of the Jalcheduns, Chemeguavas, Cocomaricopas, Pimas, Yutas, Baquiobas, Lipan Yavipais, and Natajé Yavipais, and are enemies of the Tejua Yavipais, Jamajabs, Yumas, and with good reason I can say of New Mexico also.

The Tejua Yavipais are friends of the Yumas, Jamajabs, Chemeguavas, Nabajai Yavipais, and Gileño Yavipais, and are enemies of the Jalcheduns, Gileño Pimas, Cocomaricopas, northern Yavipais, and [the Hopis of] Oraibe.

The Chemeguavas are friends of the Yutas, of all the Yavipais and all the nations to the west, and enemies of the Comanches, Hopis, and Jalcheduns.

The Indians of the Gila River are all friends among themselves and of the Jalcheduns, and enemies of the Tejuas and Apaches.

These combinations of nations show how necessary is the possession of the entire Colorado River area for the permanence of the establishments of Monterey, the Indian nations of which are united to the nations of that area; if the latter [the Indians of the Colorado] were our enemies, it would not be easy to maintain the establishments at Monterey except at great expense to the Royal Treasury; and on the other hand, whatever is spent in subduing the nations of the Colorado will help keep the missions on the coast; the mountain Indians by themselves are not worth fearing. There would thus be afforded, moreover, prompt help from the Colorado, And as the connection is quite obvious between the Apaches who harass us and some of the nations of the Colorado and the places of safety the marauders therefore have among them, we would succeed in cutting off such retreats and preventing their forays.

THIRD POINT

Nations Ready to Receive Religious Instruction and Become Subjects of His Majesty, and the Missions Needed

All the nations that live along the Gila and Colorado rivers as far as the Jamajabs, inclusive, have shown a very special liking for the Spaniards and have said (as may be seen in the Record proper) that they will willingly receive the Spaniards and the Fathers. The missions needed are: Among the Cucapá nation, two, one at Las Llagas and the other at the Laguna de San Mateo; among the Jalliquamai nation, one at Santa Rosa; among the Cajuenche nation, one at the Laguna de la Merced, another at San Francisco; among the Yuma nation, one at San Pablo, another at the Puerto de la Concepción; among the Jalchedun nation, one at San Pedro, another at San Antonio; among the Jamajab nation, one at Santa Isabel, another at La Pasión; among the nation of the Gileño Pimas, one at San Juan Capistrano, another at La Encarnación; among the Cocomaricopa nation, one at San Simón y San Judas de Upasoitac, another at San Diego de Vitorrium; among the Pápago nation, one at Sonoitac and, with good foresight, another at Atí.

FOURTH POINT

Presidios

The number and stationing of presidios and of soldiers is a matter expressly for the Viceregal Government; nevertheless, with the greatest respect, I shall express my opinion. On the supposition that His Majesty grants two presidios, respectively for the Gila and the Colorado rivers, if they are of fifty men, two missions could be maintained under the protection of each. If established downriver from the Yumas, the presidio should have an additional ten men for each mission as the necessary guard for them; if upriver from the Yumas, since it would be among the most dominating, numerous, and warlike nations, who, besides, have friends in every direction, the guard for each mission should consist of twelve men over and above those of the presidio. These men should always be at the mission, and the captain should have no authority to detail them for other duty or to reduce the number. When the men's places on the rolls are no longer needed, they should lapse in favour of the Royal Treasury or should be used in the founding of other missions. Moreover, I am of the opinion that the missions and the presidios, so far as is possible, should be placed on the far side of the river, to protect both horses and cattle from the Apaches. That nation, though not numerous, has made itself dreaded; and it is not easy to punish them because, as I have said above, they have wide cover and hustle off droves of our horses to Moqui.

The soldiers of the mission guard should be, so far as is possible, married men, because then God's work is better done.

FIFTH POINT
Means for Subduing the Apaches

In view of the short distance, as can be seen on the map, from the Gila River to Moqui, and supposing that the King our Sovereign has granted a presidio for that river and its missions, it seems to me that it might well be placed on the Río de la Asunción or, if there is one, at a better site midway between the points mentioned, so long as it is near the Tejuas. For the force at this presidio there would be required fifty leatherjackets, eighty dragoons, and fifty or more men in forced service. This presidio, having good pastureland, and providing escorts to the missions on the Gila River, will be a formidable safeguard against the Apaches, who, when harassed by us at the border, will come against it as they fall back and at little cost will be hard hit by it. At the same time, communication will be prevented between the Apaches and their friends the Tejuas, who, with so powerful a presidio menacing them, will fear to give them help. From what is written in the Record about the Yumas and their friendships it can be inferred that there will be left to the Tejuas no friends except the Apaches, granted the establishment of presidios on the Gila and Colorado rivers.

The presidio mentioned above may patrol as far as Oraibe to uncover the Apaches' designs and the part that our droves of horses have in them. It will likewise serve to assure communication between these provinces and New Mexico. It will avert any threats to the missions of the Colorado River and respect for it may give permanence to the peace that has been made. In time it may serve for the subjection of Moqui. At present the Hopi Indians, with their trade in awls, digging-sticks, grub hoes, knives, woven stuffs, and strips of red baize, are masters over all the nations; yet this presidio may humble their pride if the heathen come to it to get these things, wherefore (if we treat them as the King commands) there will again be convenience and we shall gain the advantages the Hopis now have. If trade with New Mexico is forbidden the Hopis, they will have to humble themselves and want our friendship.

This presidio can also serve to guard that better route which I have seen and travelled to Monterey, which is the following: from Chihuahua to Janos, to San Bernardino; to the junction of the Gila and San Pedro rivers; to the Asunción; [to the] Santa María; crossing the Colorado River; and from there by way of San Felipe or, crossing the mountain range of the Cajuala Chemegues' country, coming out at the same San Felipe River; or crossing the mountain range of Cailfornia through the country of the Jequiches or of the Jenigueches, and arriving at San Gabriel. All this is based on the supposition that the Apaches are under subjection or that their retreat is blocked.

I believe that on the Asunción River there will be found places suitable for crops, for use when there may not be direct access to the Gila; all on the supposition that the missions are founded. With this presidio, and with heed from New Mexico, I hope the Apaches will be conquered entirely and a stop put to the driving off northward of countless horses.

Sixth Point

Routes That May Provide Communication Between Monterey and These Provinces and New Mexico

First, I shall suppose that for the passage of seven hundred or a thousand men there is no convenient way so far as I have seen; but for a smaller number there are the two routes taken by the expeditions of years just past—the two I have described in my account of the journey to and from San Gabriel. Both are good under foot and supply forage, but are scant in water, though if the waterholes are deepened and cleaned they may provide enough.

In my opinion it is, however, better and quicker to go from the Gila River by way of the Jalcheduns' country; once the river is crossed, a day's journey away are the Tinajas de San José, a good watering-place, and from here, again a day's journey, is the land of the Jequiches, or Danzarines, where, they tell me, are marshes with reed grass and no lack of the grass the soldiers call *galleta* [army hardbread]. Thence one will come to the Puerto de San Carlos.

If one does not wish to go by this route from the beginnings of the Jequiches' country, it is possible to go along the slope of the Sierra Nevada as far as the Jenigueches' territory in the same mountain range and from there by one day's journey to the Arroyo de los Mártires, by which San Gabriel may be reached, or, if not, San Luis [Obispo] over the route followed by [Captain] Pedro Fages.

If none of these four routes will do, it is possible to go as I went, that is, by way of the route between Sonora and Monterey. If one wants to go by way of New Mexico, one can go through the Yutas' country, seeking the San Felipe River; following it down, one comes upon my route.

[95]

I have no doubt there is a better and shorter way than the one I took from Oraibe to the country of the Jalcheduns; because I went by grace of the Indians, I went where they took me, even though I knew I was going a long way round; for I must see to it that I please the Indians and that they know I am not in their lands out of curiosity, but to visit them and speak to them of good things. This I shall take up later at more length.

Seventh Point

On the Information Reported to Mexico City by
the Rev. Father Fray Silvestre de Escalante,
Missionary to Zuñi in the Year 1775

One month after returning from my travels to my mission of San Xavier del Bac, I received from His Excellency the Viceroy a letter with copy enclosed of one from the Rev. Father Fray Silvestre Vélez de Escalante, dated New Mexico, August 18, 1775. After reading carefully the report made by the Comina Indian to the Rev. Father, I must say that what it calls the Río de los Misterios is the Colorado River. To say that it cannot be crossed by the Cominas and that they do not know if there are people on the other side, I hold to be an exaggeration or a misleading comment by the Indian, for it is certain that there are people there and that they are friends of the Cominas, such as the Chemeguavas, the Sevinta Chemeguavas, and the Cajualas.

It is true that passage may be difficult upstream from the Jamajabs' country because the river flows through a narrow way with steep walls and the terrain is very rugged, but it is well known that all the Yavipais do cross it. The Cominas, as the Rev. Father calls them, may be the Jamajabs, for I heard them called by other nations "Culisnurs" or "Culisnisna"; but the Indian [who made the report] could hardly be of their rancherías, because they are enemies of the Hopis and even, until now, of all the Yavipais between. True enough, these Culisnisnas, or Jamajabs, know that there are Spaniards in these lands. I do not know that the Chidumas (who are, I think, the Yumas) eat human flesh, as the Comina Indian said. As to the mountain ranges, he is not far wrong, for the two that he mentions exist; but his report is mistaken in the directions and the the number of days.

The Rev. Father's idea of seeking a way through the Yutas' country seems to me a good one, provided it be through the lands of the Indians who live north of Moqui where the rivers join, who told me they were friends of the New Mexico Indians. Once the Colorado River is crossed, one should continue southwest, down to the territory of the Cajuala Chemeguets, then to the San Felipe River, and by it to where I was. If, from the said Yutas' country, the west-northwest route is followed, as the Rev. Father says, it is true that one could make one's way to the harbour of San Francisco and to Monterey if in between there were not, as we know, the widespreading Tulares; one can get through them only by boats. Nevertheless, by this route if one cuts [across] the big river the Noches told me about, which drains into the Tulares together with the San Felipe or very near it, one can get to the harbour of San Francisco. Monterey, however, can be reached only by making a great circuit; one would have to go downstream and avoid the marshes.

Notwithstanding, the discovery of this big river may be very useful; according to my information, it comes from the northeast, and it may be the river which the expedition led by Juan de Oñate in 1604 called the Tisón.[27] This must also be the river of which information was given in the year 1538 to the Rev. Father Juan de la Asunción when, by order of the Rev. Father Nisa, he came in by way of Sinaloa. In the report he made of his journey he says that after going six hundred leagues to the northwest of Mexico City he came to a river so big that he could not cross it; and he adds that the Indians of this river told him that ten days' journey to the north there was another, larger river, along which lived so many people that their numbers were as handfuls of sand; that they had three-storey houses; that their pueblos were walled; and that they wore clothing and footgear of deerhide and blankets of cotton.

It is my considered judgement, as I have just returned from the northeast, that since according to the information given me the ten full days' journey would bring one to the Colorado River, the Colorado was the big river which brought the Father to a halt, and there he got the further information: I am thinking now of the detail about clothing, for besides the nations that I have seen wearing deerhide and blankets the Jamajabs told me that all the nations in the north wear clothing. That there are houses and walled settlements is easy to believe when one has seen Moqui, where the houses are two and three

---

27. Father Garcés was much mistaken in trying to relate these two rivers. Juan de Oñate, in 1604-1605, went down the lower Colorado River, already called the Río del Tisón; but he did not go up into the great valley of California, where Garcés' "big river" was. Pedro de Castañeda's account of the Coronado expedition of 1540-1542 says (p. 485 in G. P. Winship's translation): "On account of the great cold [the Indians] carry a firebrand *(tisón)* in the hand when they go from one place to another, with which they warm the other hand and the body as well, and in this way they keep shifting it every now and then. On this account the large river in that country was called the Río del Tisón ('Firebrand River')." Capt. Lorenzo Sitgreaves' *Report of an Expedition down the Zuñi and Colorado Rivers* records (p. 18) that "the custom still [1851] prevails among them."

storeys high, and on the side where I entered, as they had neither doors nor windows, they looked more like walls than houses. I hold, therefore, as quite credible the information given in the account mentioned.

I find information about this river also in the account of the expedition of Captain Francisco Vásquez de Coronado, undertaken in the year 1540 by order of the Viceroy, Antonio de Mendoza. I consider this account truthful because I have seen almost everything it speaks of. The pueblo of Bacapá which it mentions is found today in Papaguería, with the name of Quitobac. *Apa* in the Pima language is 'in', *bac* is 'reed', and so Quitobac means 'among small reeds'. The Río de las Balsas that he mentions is the Colorado River. He says that going to the north, with some deviations, they came to the "Alchedom" nation; by the same route I came to the one I call the Jalchedun. All that it says about the sea is true; small vessels are found in the [Santa Barbara] Channel. The scent of copal I too remarked on my journey—though it may not have been precisely copal. The people whom they saw, some with wavy, some with straight hair, I too have seen; and their pointing west when describing their land may have been toward the island of Santa Cruz (even though they might not have seen it, nor those of the Channel, as happens today if there is fog). The *pavellones* [light outdoor structures] which the account says they saw in this land have much in common with those of sewn rushes which I saw when among the Cuabajais and mention in my Record.

The account also tells that they reached the river near Moqui and after six days' journey arrived at the Llanos de la Cíbola, inhabited by the nation they called Vaqueros ['cowboys']. When I was among the Yavipais near Moqui, I was told of a nation they call Baquioba, which is evidently the same people as the Vaqueros of the account, for they too pointed them out to me as in the north. The flax and hemp which the account mentions that they saw, I too have said I found. Granting, then, that up to this point I find the account agreeing so well with what I have seen, I give the same credence to what follows, which is, that from the place where they crossed into the nation of the Vaqueros the soldiers left toward the north and after six days' journey discovered, on the banks of a great river, a large city with three-storey houses surrounded by high walls; they saw it from a hilltop near the large settlement, called Quivira, of the Tejua nation.

In my humble opinion, this and the other report are true and not only does a great river exist, but also the large settlements mentioned. The same has been said, in part, by an Apache of this province.

[98]

With this information, and that which I have about the Comanches, plus the knowledge, which I have mentioned, that the Chemeguavas as well as the Yutas are their enemies, it is my opinion that the people of this great river, and they that live in those large settlements, are the Comanches; for I know that in Texas they have said that they come from far away and set out from a very large river. Consequently it would not be a bad idea, before undertaking any expedition, to conclude peace with them when they come to Texas to trade their deerhides. For such an expedition, it seems to me, at least eighty men with two priests are needed. They should have some awls, strips of red cloth, red being the colour that pleases the Indians most, and other knicknacks to use as presents and for trading. Our men should not be permitted to give the slightest offense, nor should the Indians be cheated in the trading, all of which should be done in the presence of the head [of the expedition]. If any member of such an expedition does wrong, he should be punished in the presence of the Indians, to make amends to them. I am obliged to suggest such a measure because of the strong complaints which, as I have said, were addressed to me by the Noches and Cuabajais.

If command of this river may be assured, then in case it is possible to go down to the reed marshes in small boats and through them to the harbour of San Francisco, it will be helpful for trade even with China; for, once the Manila Galleon comes to San Francisco, the missions of New Mexico and of the interior will be able to supply themselves by way of the Tulares and the great river. These interior provinces will be happy if trade with China be made possible by way of this river, and with Spain by way of the Mississippi.

Eighth Point
Equipping the Missions

Since I was for the first time in San Gabriel and saw the needs of those missions [i.e., the missions of Upper California], I have thought about equipping the missions of the Colorado River and its presidio, when they may be founded, and I find difficulties always. However, leaving that for the present to those who are to consider it more fully, I shall give my opinion about equipping these establishments by sea and by land.

Once the land is pacified, as I hope it will be in consequence of the steps taken toward that end, the land route may be: from Chihuahua to Janos, to San Bernardino, to Santa Cruz, to the Gila River, and down to the Yumas; if not, to the presidio on the Asunción and by way of the Santa María to the Colorado.

However, considering that this route, taken from Mexico City, is of more than six hundred leagues' distance, with no few difficulties and the hazards of some unrest in the nations that lie along the way, and lastly because of the great cost to the missions and presidios, I shall speak of the way by sea.

This route may be either by way of the Gulf of California or by way of the South Sea [Pacific Ocean] and the harbour of San Diego. If through the Gulf, the journey should be made in a small vessel with sails and oars, at the seasons known from experience to be favourable. If the boat could go upriver as far as the Yuma country, to unload right at the presidio and the missions, nothing could be more advantageous; if not, were a mission to be founded among the Cucapás the supplies could be discharged at the creeks and inlets of that shore and later taken to the proper destinations by pack trains. That the boat must be a small one seems to me no obstacle to equipping all the missions; for a few years they will only need cloth, coarse brown sugar, and other small supplies. If even this should seem difficult, orders could be given for the vessels that supply the establishments at Monterey to take the things for the Colorado River to the harbour of San Diego, where, if there were a warehouse in which to store such cargo, it could later be sent on by pack train. For this, it would seem to me that the detachment at San Diego should be subject to the commander or captain of the Colorado River [district], for many good reasons: first, for quickest aid in case of need, since it is nearest the River and Monterey; secondly, because the road from San Diego to the Colorado River is safer than that to Monterey when the intervening nations are caught between the two forces; thirdly, because the complaints and quarrels among the Indians of the [Santa Barbara] Channel will probably be fewer if they do not go over to Monterey so frequently; fourthly, the advantage of a supply of provisions, should there be need of them upon the return of the pack trains.

For all these reasons and others I do not mention, I believe such subordination of command to be advisable. If it does not exist, disagreements may arise among the commanding officers which may hamper the [proposed] foundations on the Colorado River. Another good reason that I see for sending equipment through San Diego is that in the event some nation or nations on the land route should take up arms and prevent passage, they would not be able to cut communication with the Colorado River by sea.

In view of what the first Spaniards did, of what the next omitted to do, and of what is now planned to be done, I can do no less than give many thanks to

God. The first Spaniards began to give religious instruction in Sinaloa, made discoveries as far as the seacoast, and glimpsed the land of Quivira, which some have held to be imaginary, whereas now, from what we know of Moqui, it seems real. During the past century the Faith has been spread in these provinces, yet I see that despite peaceful times without enemies and without greater expense to the Royal Treasury than for the presidio of Janos, results have been nil. It is because of this failure in conquering souls for God and provinces for the Sovereign, when the docility of so many neighbouring nations was inviting us to do so, that I fear God permitted the fury of the Apaches to prevent us not only from going further, but from increasing the strength of the old foundations, forcing us to use up many lives and much property in defensive war alone. If the money spent in containing these enemies since they began to attack (or since God took them as an instrument for punishing our sins) had been spent on new establishments, where would not now be planted the Christian standard? In how many provinces as yet unknown would not our Sovereign be obeyed?

Thanks be to God, I see reviving in our time the old Spanish passion for discovering and taking possession of new lands in order to gather precious pearls, the souls of men! Recently new coasts of the South Sea have been discovered, as far as that much talked of but never sufficiently praised harbour of San Francisco, where now at last praise is offered to our mighty God, and our men are going even further up the coast with Christian valour. I see the great steps that are being taken for having us press further into the interior, and I firmly believe that God will favour our enterprise by bringing to us the most savage nations, if we please Him by adding at once to His church so many thousands of souls as today are disposed to join it, and are awaiting us with open arms, as can be seen in my Record.

When I heard the statement of the King our Sovereign in his decree concerning new Rules and Regulations, in these or similar words: that "as one of the things that most occupy my Royal attention is the conversion of the heathen, I direct my Viceroy to inform me whether any nation or nations wish to join our religion," [28] I became convinced that undoubtedly his Royal heart will be pleased when he sees that so many nations named in this Record have shown an intense desire to receive the Faith and to be subjects of His Majesty.

---

28. This is not a verbatim quotation, but a reminder of the King's wishes and intentions. The "Rules and Regulations" referred to are embodied in the *Reglamento e Instrucción* of 1772, for which see *The Coming of Justice to California*, edited by John Galvin (1963).

Furthermore, I am certain that toward this end our Sovereign will omit nothing necessary, even at very great increase of expense. For we who have the good fortune to be subjects of so great a King have come to know his pious disposition of wanting more souls for God than riches for his Royal Treasury. This, no doubt, is what assures him so much glory in one world and the other, and, after this life, in Heaven.

I end thus: The King our Sovereign wishes; the King our Sovereign can do it; therefore, the King our Sovereign will do it at once, since it is so virtuous and befitting a thing. Amen.

I solemnly affirm that in everything I have said in the Record and in the Reflections added to it, only the honour and glory of God impels me. I do not intend to prejudice the opinion of anyone. I have been voicing with Christian candour what I have grasped, relating without distortion what I have seen and heard and laid my hand upon which may perhaps serve as a guide to the decisions the Viceregal Government may wish to make. I am well aware that my want of energy, my many defects, and the sins I have probably committed, on this and other occasions when I have gone into heathen territory, must partly, perhaps wholly, bear the blame that more has not as yet been done; but it gives me some comfort that the way is open and we can go in to reap the harvest and that if it is not gathered it will be solely because labourers are not sent.

In this Record many failings are apparent; I can only acknowledge that all are from lack of more capacity. If any discrepancies are found between it and the map in number of leagues, routes, and bearings, the map must always have priority because it was drawn after the Record was written; and when it was necessary to correct anything, even though the changes were of little importance, it was done in my presence. The numbers that were promised for the days' journeys had been omitted, but are in this copy.

Fr. Franco Garcés

Tubutama, January 3, 1777

39

38

37

S. Feè.

R. Grande.

Yutas. Mòqui Zuñi

Òraibe. Sierra delos Mimbres 36

R. des Antteno Jabessua
Cuercomaches. Sierra de Mogollòn 35

R. de S. Bernabè A P A C

Yabipais cajuala R. dela Assumpc.

Laguayepais R. de S. Francisco. Arrete de Mimbres

ta Maria R. Gila H E R I A. 34

R. de S. Ybapais (e) ua Apach S. Marcial.

Pimas. R. de S. Pedro Chiricagat. 33

Cocomaricopas

Tuquison S. Cruz. S. Bernardino. Janos. 32

Sonotac GUE RIA. Tubac. Calabas. Cocospera Cuquiarachi Fronteras

Jutotac. Saric. Tubutama Ati Altar Pitiqui Terrenate Dolor Bacuachi 31

Bisani S. Ygn. Dolor Chinapa N O R A.

Caborca S. Ana Tuape Arispe Cune pas Guavabas

Pimer ia Alta Opodepe Bananchi Ope sura

Nacameri Aconchi 30

Cieneguilla Babiacora Basaracas

S O Bacadeguac hi

Y. de el Tiburon S. Mig.l Vres Batuco

S. Jose Alamo 29

Matape

Patiqui Nacori

Pimeria Teopari Natora

S. Aribechi

Tecoripa Onapa Taruqui 28

S. Marcial Baja R. chico

Cumuripa Mobas Yecora Maicoba

Buenavista Prov. DE Ostimuri. 27

Pto de Guaimas Pue blos de Yaqui Baroyeca
Batocosa
Tepague

R. Yaqui

Conicari 26

Real delos Alamos

GOLFO DE CALIFORNIAS.

NIA.

TULARES

Agua Dulce

Pto. de S. Fran.co

Monterrey

R. de Monterrey

S. Ant.o

Sta Cruz
R. de S.tiago
R. de S. Felipe.

S. Luis

Nochis.

Tabajas

Chemegues

Arroyo delos Martires
Jamajabas.

S. Gabriel

R. COLOR.

Canal de Sta. Barbara

S. Carlos

Jalchedunes.

Yumas

Pto. n
de S. Diego

Cajuenches.

PA

La del Angel custodio
Canal de Ballenas

CALIFOR.

PLANO

Que conti.e las Provincias de Sonora, Pimerias, Papagueria Apache-
ria, Rios Gila, y Colorado, y tierras descubiert.s hasta el Puerto de S.
Fran.co en la california Septembrional y hasta el Pueblo de Oraybe n
en la Provincia de el Moqui, con arreglo a los diarios de el coronel D.n
Ant.o Crespo y de los PP. Misioner.s Fr. Pedro Font, y Fr. Fran.co Garces de q.e los
viajes desde la nacion Tabajaba en el Rio Colorado hasta la Mision de S.n
Gabriel, a las naciones que estan al Norte de esta Mision, su regreso a las
Jamajabas, y camino que hizo al Moqui estan señalados con lineas de pun-
tos: con cuia Señal se manifiesta tambien la linea de Presidios de es-
ta frontera.
  Los Presidios se notan con esta Señal .... ✠
  Los Reales de minas, y Placer.s Poblad.s .... ⊕
  Los demas Pueblos de cristianos .... ⊙
  Los Pueblos de Ynfiel.s y aguajes de las tierr.s de estos .... ⊙

MAR PACIFICO.

5 10 15 20 25

Leguas de 17½ en grado

MAP embracing the Provinces of Sonora, the Pimerías, Papaguería, Apachería, the Gila and Colorado rivers, and lands discovered as far as the harbour of San Francisco in northern California and as far as the pueblo of Oraibe in the Province of Moqui, in agreement with the diaries of Colonel Antonio Crespo and the missionary priests Father Pedro Font and Father Francisco Garcés, whose travels from the territory of the Jamajab Indians on the Colorado River as far as San Gabriel Mission and to the lands of the Indians north of that mission, their return to the land of the Jamajabs, and the way to Moqui, are indicated by rows of dots, with which there is shown also the line of presidios of this frontier.

Presidios are indicated by this symbol . . . . ⚲

Mining towns and inhabited places . . . . ⚲

Other settlements of Christians . . . . ⚲

Indian villages, and watering-places in their lands . . . . ⊙

[NOTE: The summary given above corrects Father Garcés' statement in his "Preliminary Remarks" that "on the map the entire route is shown by dots." The map does not show his line of travel with the expedition from Tubac to the Yuma crossing, nor that of his excursion to the mouth of the Colorado River, nor that of his return home from the Yuma crossing again; these routes will be found on another map, specially drawn for this book. Moreover, Father Font did not accompany Father Garcés on the route "shown by dots"; he continued with Anza's expedition. Governor Crespo of Sonora suggested routes but did not make the journey. The "line of presidios" shown is too rigidly straight and is incomplete.]

APPENDICES

Letter from His Excellency the Viceroy, Antonio de Bucareli,
to Father Francisco Garcés

In a communication dated May 3 last I am informed, on the King's instructions, by the illustrious José de Gálvez as follows:

"Through Your Excellency's letter of January 27 of this year, and through one from Father Garcés which you enclosed, the King has learned with great satisfaction of the reports which this priest gives of his journeys from the Colorado River to San Gabriel Mission and thence to Moqui, making his way through tribes hitherto unknown. His Majesty awaits the travel diary which has been prepared for the Royal service and commands that in his Royal name Your Excellency should thank Father Garcés for the zeal and fervour with which he is endeavouring to acquire knowledge of, deal with, and draw in, tribes so little known."

Which Royal wish I communicate to Your Reverence, thanking you in the King's name for the tenacity with which you unsparingly devote yourself to introducing into places so remote the seed of the Gospel and dependence upon the Sovereign. May God preserve Your Reverence many years.

Mexico City, August 9, 1777.   Bucareli

A Sermon delivered at the Colegio de la Santa Cruz, Querétaro, July 19, 1794, by Father Bringas de Manzaneda, honouring the memory of Fathers Garcés, Díaz, Moreno, and Barreneche, missionaries from that seminary, who were slain at their mission-posts on the lower Colorado River by hostile Indians July 17 and 19, 1781

We should not shed tears of inconsolable grief at the death of the just. Religion's heroes, those chosen ones who proceed from the bosom of the Almighty, whom with His potent hand from time to time He shapes as models for our emulation, are useful to religion and to us in life and death alike.

Were there lacking in our hearts the dear resource of a consoling hope, to nourish those impulses which lift our spirits heavenward, and to sustain us amidst life's afflictions, then indeed we should, like pagans, permit the harmony of our being to break beneath the pressures of a comfortless sorrow. That hope banishes from my heart all importunate distress.

Yet how can I look unmoved on the sacrifice of four priests who were as so many pillars upon which rested the most substantial expectancies of this Seminary? In that sepulchral urn, its only pomp the humble neatness of Franciscan poverty, there rest the ashes, deserving respect, of Fray Juan Marcelo Díaz; there, sundered, the remains of Fray José Matías Moreno, whose skull perchance the savages keep as a testimony of their ingratitude. Fray Juan Antonio de Barreneche, splendid youth, escapes not my memory. Nor Fray Francisco Garcés; merely to view his glorious deeds confounds me, makes me feel that time is all too short for reciting merits that only silent admiration could encompass. Subject to the judgement of Holy Church, I am emboldened to propose that the worthy Father Garcés and his companions have, in God's sight, the merit of true martyrs.

Just as, in the words of St. Paul, the sun, the moon, and the stars have each a different splendour, so, my hearers, you shall behold shining like the sun among the planets that remarkable man whom I but now mentioned. Grant me, I pray you, the honour of your attention, that I may give you even an imperfect portrayal of that extraordinary man, that incomparable missionary, that dauntless heart, the worthy Father Francisco Garcés. But how shall I depict for you the great soul of this apostolic minister? How shall I give you an adequate idea of his most amiable self?

Lacking as I am in the inspiration of the missionary spirit, I can only address you worthily by letting myself be led in fancy along the winding banks of the flowing Colorado River, eagerly and devotedly to gain some measure of the spirit that animated our worthy brothers in that region. Truly, when, filled with an ecstasy of wonder and gladness, I transport myself as in a vision to the most distant parts of our America, my heart in dread goes tumbling round and nowhere can regain its calm. I go even to the land of Moqui, sometimes with satisfaction most complete, imagining that I see it circled by a poor Franciscan like Jerusalem by the zealous Nehemiah, with Providence his only store, faith his only guard, and borne in upon him from the record of past years that the object of all the thwarted endeavours of sagacious and earnest missionaries spurred on by the repeated injunctions of the Kings of Spain could only be attained by a missionary of this Seminary; at other times I think on the heedfulness with which the new missionaries to those regions strive, perhaps at this very moment, to discover traces by which they may find marked out for them the path trod by the worthy Father Garcés; and at yet other times, filled with sentiments of compassion, I reflect upon those troops of savages who wander through the thickets or stand menaced by the shadows of darkness and death.

How great the weariness [of those four missionaries]! They could have only broken slumbers, subject at any moment to alarms. They had to make up with mere snatches of rest for the strains of travelling hundreds of leagues through barren lands peopled only by savages: Barreneche, more than three hundred leagues; Moreno, more than four hundred; Díaz, more than seven hundred; and Garcés, more than two thousand—to adopt only the most moderate estimates, which refer, moreover, just to their travels among the heathen. Theirs was to preach the Gospel; but in that ministry how hard was their lot in comparison with ours! We compose our discourses in the midst of peace, sheltered by a silence over which our discipline keeps watchful guard, enlightened through the aid of many thousands of volumes in our library, borne up by the promptings of many subjects well capable of lifting from our shoulders a good part of our weight of weariness; and, above all, filled with a favourable expectation that the town which hears us speak will give us heed, will respect our priestly character (we giving more than sufficiently good cause that it should be venerated), almost will reverence our persons by reason of whatever grounds for esteem we have inherited from our betters, partly from those hallowed ashes of which we speak today, those men whose spirit we must be eager to regain. But those four missionaries at the very first step of their preaching missions were cumbered with the dullest and most meagrely rewarding of employments, the rude task of learning a harsh and irregular mode of expression and of pronouncing several barbarous tongues, laying themselves open to the mockery of the lowest heathen, gathering instead of plaudits only confusion and embarrassment inasmuch as they were not masters of a strange style of speech; finally winning through by virtue of prodigious efforts, of fervent good-will, and of untiring tenacity.

Filling out twelve years in his last mission area, in which no minister had been able to endure for more than a single year, Father Garcés lived in it like a very Apostle, with no other bed than the ground, no covering but his habit, no other table than Providence supplied, and with the plainest of fare, as insipid as herbage: parched corn, or cornmeal, and other food of the sort, such as the savages have, with whom he lived familiarly so far as decency would permit. I shall say nothing of that generosity with which he would share with the Indians the scant supply allotted to him for his own needs: leaf tobacco or snuff, neither of which did he ever himself use; and chocolate, which was not for him to breakfast on.[1] Nor shall I speak of how he resigned himself many a time on his wide travels to eating mice and small lizards, squirrels, seeds of grasses, the roots of the rushes commonly called tules, juniper berries, and perchance, because at the last extremity of need, the loathsome flesh of a horse.

Father Garcés was killed by powerful and merciless blows from barbarous hands, at the vigorous age of forty-three, in the best of health, at the height of his career.

Imagine two small settlements newly established beside the flowing Colorado River, surrounded by three thousand barbarians plotting their destruction, each settlement attended by two ministers who are spending the daylight hours in the wastes, summoning the heathen flock to religious instruction. This was the situation on the 17th of July, 1781, nine months after their establishment: the savages came as a dense cloud and with horrible ferocity assailed the mission-post of Fathers Garcés and Barreneche; the latter had just concluded a Mass; the former was just beginning his, but on hearing the howls of the barbarians and the pitiful cries of their victims the mission-dwellers, he broke off. Yes, the dread shape of death showed itself to these two just men with all the horrors that could daunt the most intrepid soul. The illustrious young Barreneche went

---

1. Alexander Forbes, *California*, p. 115, noting a remark of Anza's that "there was not so much as a cup of chocolate to enable [the Spaniards at Monterey] to break their fast," adds: "a privation, of all others the most insufferable to a Mexican Spaniard, to whom chocolate is one of the most indispensable necessaries of life."

out from the small church to receive the last sighs of the dying, and, oblivious of the cruel blows showered on him by the barbarians, he managed to hear, absolve, and console as many as he could. This onslaught being entirely a consequence of wanton barbarism, the attacking Indians withdrew from the little settlement and scattered through the neighbouring fields, some of them slaying Christians whom they took unawares among the thickets, while a large number attacked the other small settlement, whose ministers had just said Mass and were preparing to give the Holy Viaticum to a woman who was ill. All in a moment, the savages in their fury slew the mission-dwellers, set fire to the church, with cruel blows beat the last breath from the worthy Father Juan Díaz and sated their bloodthirstiness by cruelly beheading the worthy Father Moreno with a hatchet, leaving both corpses stretched upon the ground.

The worthy Fathers Garcés and Barreneche decided to abandon the place but not their flock: on the 18th of July, leading what remained of their congregation, they set off seeking the desert places. And here you shall see a shining example of the heroic benevolence of these venerable ministers; for on reaching the edge of a sheet of water, of a depth to suit its broad expanse, they heard on the far side a mortally wounded Spanish soldier crying out in anguish; whereupon the worthy Father Barreneche, indifferent to the manifest peril of drowning, the fervour of his charity not permitting him so much as to cast aside his robe and sandals, plunged fearlessly into the water with his breviary in one hand and a crucifix in the other, to relieve the sufferer; a while, he battled with death in the water, but with God's help he made the further shore, where he heard, consoled, and absolved the dying man. Meanwhile the worthy Father Garcés presented a most glorious spectacle: determined though he was to follow his comrade through the same dangers, he must first give an earnest of his charity. Among those who came following were some that were almost naked, and in order to relieve their need he took off his robe and his habit and divided these among them; then, wearing only his shirt and cowl, he plunged into the water. Reunited, the two priests took refuge in the dwelling-place of a heathen, where on the following day, the 19th of July, they were surprised by a crowd of savages who were looking for them, not to kill them, but to take them to the midmost part of their nation.

But here you must refresh your recollection of what I have already suggested to you; that is, that these four zealous ministers died as oblations offered up for charity. For when these two were found, the cry of an apostate among the Indians was their death sentence, uttered thus: "If these live, these who are the

[109]

worst of all, then everything is lost." While this savage cry, which was a most eloquent tribute to the merits of these two heroes, was still echoing, merciless blows rained upon them until they were dead, leaving the few that remained of their little flock as captives among the barbarians.

In this pitiful manner the last breath was driven from four upstanding, vigorous, healthy missionaries in the prime of their lives, glowing with their souls' devotion, heirs of a spirit like that of the Apostles.

May their souls repose in the everlasting tabernacles of peace. Amen.

GLOSSARY

aguaje, a watering-place.

alcalde, in an Indian community, an official subordinate to the local ruler (*gobernador*).

aliso, alder tree.

arroyo, watercourse, wet or dry.

balsa, Indian boat made of reeds.

cañada, small valley, usually with a watercourse and some vegetation.

ciénaga, marsh, with or without open water.

custodio (custodian), superior of a group of Franciscan monasteries of lesser status than a province.

guardián, local superior of a Franciscan monastery.

laguna, pond, pool, rain pool, body of standing water, according to the context; at any rate, a watering-place for men and animals.

machete, heavy straight-backed blade for cutting underbrush, etc.

mescal, food or drink prepared from the maguey plant, the American agave; Garcés specifically mentions it as food.

mesquites, mesquite shrubs: the flat-pod and the screwbean, which supplied the Indians with much food.

pinabetes, conifers, including yellow pines, firs, and cypress trees like those of Monterey.

pinales, pine groves.

pozo, waterhole; not a well in the sense of a stone-built structure.

presidio, garrison-post.

pueblo, village; specifically, in Hopi Indian country, a village of earthen or stone houses.

puerto, in mountains, a pass, or passage for a stream or river; at sea level, a navigable passage, or a harbour or seaport.

ranchería, Indian dwelling-place; a single hut or a group of huts; may include cultivated land.

tinaja, large earthenware water-jar; hence applied to natural basins.

tortilla, a thin flat unleavened baked pancake of mashed Indian corn.

tulares, places where tules grow.

tules, rushes, taller than a man, which grow thickly in swampy bottomland; specifically, in the areas flooded by the San Joaquin River in the great valley of California—areas once much greater than they are now.

REFERENCES

Arricivita, Juan Domingo. *Crónica seráfica y apostólica del Colegio de propaganda fide de la Santa Cruz de Querétaro en la Nueva España* (Mexico City, 1792).

Bancroft, Hubert H. *History of Arizona and New Mexico, 1530-1888* (San Francisco, 1889).

———— *History of California*, Vol. I: *1542-1800* (San Francisco, 1884).

———— *History of the North Mexican States and Texas*, Vol. I: *1531-1800* (San Francisco, 1884).

Bolton, Herbert Eugene, ed. and trans. *Anza's California Expeditions*, including *Font's Complete Diary* (Berkeley, 1930).

———— "Father Escobar's Relation of the Oñate Expedition to California, 1605," in *Catholic Historical Review*, Vol. V (1919).

Bringas de Manzaneda y Encinas, Fr. Diego Miguel. *Sermón que . . . en obsequio de* [Garcés, Díaz, Moreno, Barreneche] *. . . dixo el 19 de Julio de 1794* (Madrid, 1819).

Coues, Elliott, ed. and trans. *On the Trail of a Spanish Pioneer: The Diary and Itinerary of Francisco Garcés on His Travels through Sonora, Arizona, and California, 1775-1776* (New York, 1900).

Crespo, Francisco Antonio. "Informe que hizo al Virrey el Gobernador de Sonora acerca del descubrimiento de Monterrey para Nuevo México," dated Altar, December 15, 1774; MS in the Mexican National Archives. For an English translation see Bolton, *Anza's California Expeditions*, Vol. V, pp. 238-248.

Dutton, Clarence E. *Tertiary History of the Grand Cañon District* (2 vols. with atlas; Washington, D. C., 1882). The atlas includes panoramic views by William Henry Holmes, sketched by him in 1880.

Emory, Maj. William H. *Notes of a Military Reconnaissance from Fort Leavenworth . . . to San Diego . . . Made in 1846-7* (Washington, D. C., 1848).

———— and others. *Report on the United States and Mexican Boundary Survey* (Washington, D. C., 1857-1859). Includes lithographs from drawings of of Indians by Arthur Schott.

Forbes, Alexander. *California: A History of Upper and Lower California* (London, 1839). The first book published in English relating exclusively to California.

Ives, Lieut. Joseph C. *Report upon the Colorado River of the West, Explored in 1857 and 1858* (Washington, D. C., 1861).

Kroeber, A. L. *Handbook of the Indians of California* (Washington, D. C., 1925).

———— *Yuman Tribes of the Lower Colorado* (Berkeley, 1920).

Mindeleff, Victor. "A Study of Pueblo Architecture: Tusayan and Cíbola," in *8th Annual Report of the Bureau of Ethnology* (Washington, D. C., 1891).

Sitgreaves, Capt. Lorenzo. *Report of an Expedition down the Zuñi and Colorado Rivers* (Washington, D. C., 1853).

Spier, Leslie. *Yuman Tribes of the Gila River* (Chicago, 1933).

Van Dyke, Dix. "A Modern Interpretation of the Garcés Route," in *Annual Publications of the Historical Society of Southern California*, Vol. XIII (1927), pp. 353-359, with map.

Whipple, Lieut. A. W., and others. *Report of Explorations for a Railway Route, near the Thirty-fifth Parallel . . . from the Mississippi River to the Pacific Ocean* (Washington, D. C., 1854).

Winship, George Parker. "The Coronado Expedition, 1540-1542," in *14th Annual Report of the Bureau of Ethnology* (Washington, D. C., 1896). Includes Spanish text and English translation of Pedro de Castañeda's "Relación de la Jornada de Cíbola."

INDEX

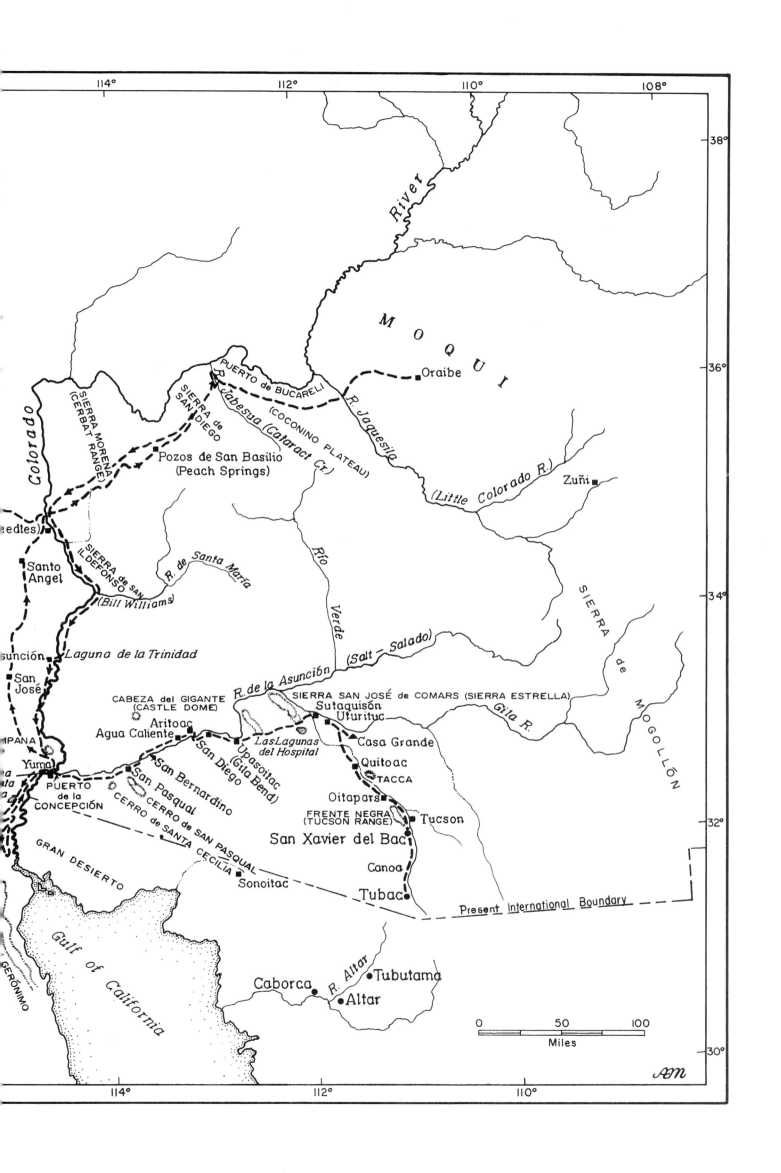

38°

36°

M O Q U I

PUERTO de BUCARELI
■ Oraibe

R. Jaquesila

Zuñi ■

(Little Colorado R.)

SIERRA MORENA
(CERBAT RANGE)

SIERRA de
SAN DIEGO

R. Jabesua (Cataract Cr.)

(COCONINO PLATEAU)

Colorado

■ Pozos de San Basilio
(Peach Springs)

(eedles) ■

SIERRA de SAN
ILDEFONSO

R. de Santa María

Río

■ Santo
Angel

(Bill Williams)

Verde

SIERRA

34°

sunción

Laguna de la Trinidad

(Salt – Salado)

de

■ San
José

R. de la Asunción

R. de la Asunción

MOGOLLÓN

CABEZA del GIGANTE
(CASTLE DOME)

SIERRA SAN JOSÉ de COMARS (SIERRA ESTRELLA)

Sutaquisón
Ufurituc

Gila R.

IPANA

Aritoac ●
Agua Caliente

Upasoitac
(Gila Bend)

LasLagunas
del Hospital

■ Casa Grande

Yuma

San Diego

Quitoac
●TACCA

PUERTO
de la
CONCEPCIÓN

San Bernardino

CERRO de SAN PASQUAL

Oitapars ■

a
ta
a

San Pasqual

CERRO de SANTA CECILIA

FRENTE NEGRA
(TUCSON RANGE)

■ Tucson

32°

San Xavier del Bac

GRAN DESIERTO

Sonoitac ■

Canoa ■

Present International Boundary

Tubac ●

GERÓNIMO

Gulf of California

Caborca ●

R. Altar

● Tubutama

● Altar

0   50   100
Miles

30°

114°   112°   110°   108°

114°   112°   110°

æm

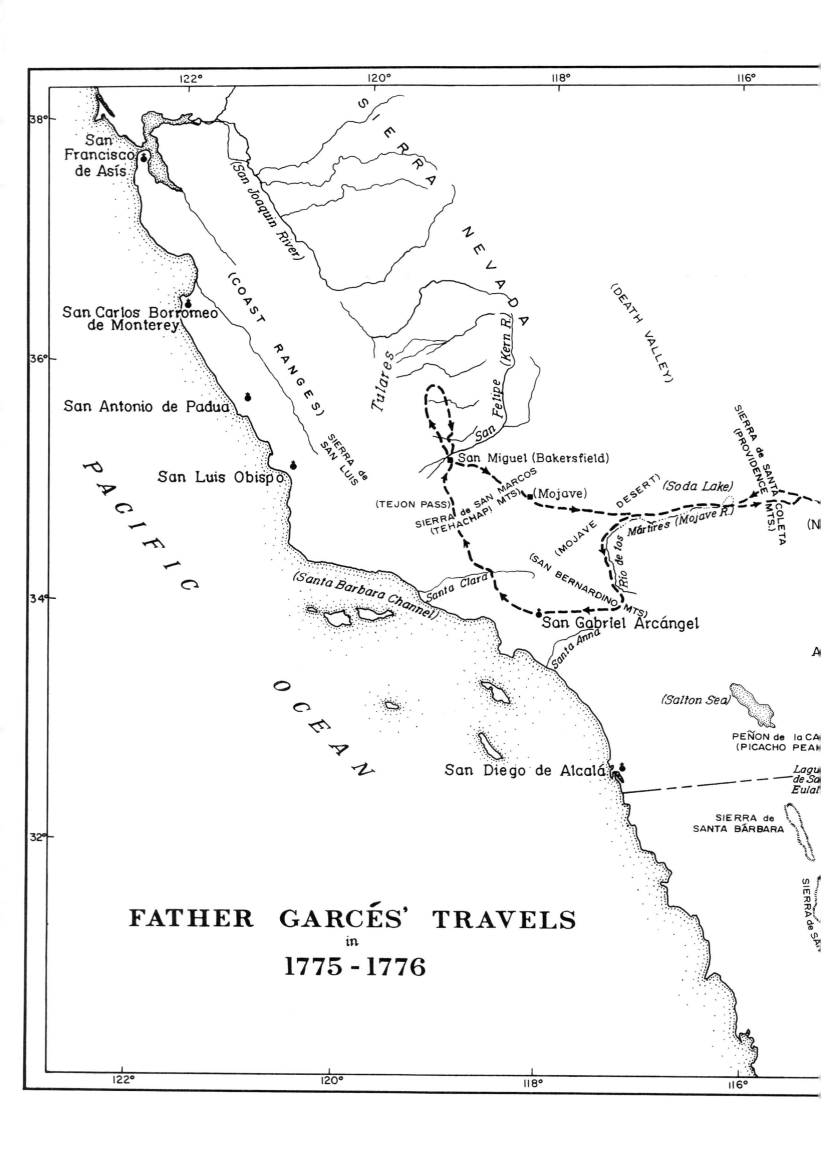

FATHER GARCÉS' TRAVELS
in
1775 - 1776